Margaret Gregg Mordecai

A Key to the Orient

Margaret Gregg Mordecai

A Key to the Orient

ISBN/EAN: 9783741132315

Manufactured in Europe, USA, Canada, Australia, Japa

Cover: Foto ©Andreas Hilbeck / pixelio.de

Manufactured and distributed by brebook publishing software (www.brebook.com)

Margaret Gregg Mordecai

A Key to the Orient

A Key to the Orient

By

Mrs. Clapham Pennington

Philadelphia:
JOHN J. McVEY.

AUTHOR'S PREFACE

THE Orient to most people of the Occident is a sealed book.

Works there are indeed, and by the greatest scholars, on the Oriental Religions; and others, though very few, of the history of oriental lands; and books of oriental travels describing the general aspect of the countries, the outside of the houses, the scenes in the streets, but leaving the inside life, the real thought and feeling of the people, dark.

But our people are not interested. The resignation and charmed calm of the Orient are too unlike the restless discontent and perpetual motion of the Occident.

The West does not understand the East, and does not wish or try to understand.

Author's Preface

But at the same time, she criticises her, and severely, judging everything by her own standards, making no allowance for difference of nature, custom, tradition, thought, and feeling, but saying it is so here, and it must be so there.

The English drink pale ale in India, saying it suits in England, therefore it must suit here. Carlsbad and Vichy tell the end of the tale, and many an Indian cemetery besides; and as long as the West judges the East by herself, she will be always in the wrong.

It is my hope in this little book to try and make people take interest in the East, and think of it as it really is. This is an humble effort, but perhaps it will lead others to study for themselves.

And one thing I can claim. I know the real life of the East, not as one knows it who walks in the streets, but as one who has been behind the lattices.

Most oriental travellers are men, and

Author's Preface

therefore the inside life is absolutely closed to them; and they would do better to pass it over in silence, for in relating from hearsay they make many mistakes.

And of the women who at present give us accounts of the East, the majority are missionaries, and with all due respect, their view of oriental life is not always one which other people would take, and liable to be, one may say, made to order.

I know the inside life of the East, first, from oriental literature, and then from what I have seen, for I have been most fortunate in having had access to oriental homes from the highest to the lowest.

I love to tell of what I have seen, and I could tell much more; but unless one enters into the thought and feeling of the East one hardly understands, and I do not wish to be misunderstood.

We must learn, first, that things are not the same everywhere. Musk in our own country is a vulgar and objectionable per-

Author's Preface

fume. But under skies to which ours are pale, and amid colors beside which ours are faded, with the jewels and the tinsel of the Orient, musk is sweet.

And so with all things. But I have found a pleasure so intense in my oriental studies and my oriental experiences that I want to share it with other people. There are many books far beyond mine which they may read, if they can be persuaded. There is much for them to see and hear, many pleasures and surprises in store for them.

But I will hope that for some at least my little book may be — a key to the Orient.

MARGARET PENNINGTON.

Contents

	PAGE
THE WOMEN OF ISLAM	3
ORIENTAL SLAVERY	75
THE MISSIONARIES AS THEY APPEAR TO THE HEATHEN	89
A BIRD'S EYE VIEW OF THE RELIGIONS OF THE ORIENT	103
THE RELIGION OF ZARATHUSTRA SPITAMA	139

The Women of Islam

THE WOMEN OF ISLAM

Part I

THE sacred fires on the altars of Iran went out on the night when Mohammed was born; and the painted Saints of the Eastern Empire may well have turned pale in their gilded shrines, for that hour was the beginning of their fall and of a series of events the most remarkable that the world has ever seen.

How little we, so-called Christians,—for God alone knows how many of us are unworthy of the name,—know of Mohammed and his wonderful life and work.

Mohammed, to whom we deny inspiration, and yet to whom amidst rank idolatry

A Key to the Orient

the knowledge of one God and truth and justice came. Mohammed, who was not afraid to speak, and whose first words aroused such a storm of indignation among his townsmen as had nearly cost him his life.

Driven from Mecca like a wild beast, we find him again in the desert, outlawed and abandoned by his kind, but not alone, the hosts of the Jinn (spirits of the air) crowding round him to listen to the word of God, which man had refused to hear.

Mohammed! who a few years later saw Arabia kneel and hail him the Prophet of God, and whose followers to-day number two hundred millions.

And who of all these millions was the first to believe? Woman, "last at the cross and first at the sepulchre," was also the first in Islam. Kadijah, Mohammed's faithful wife, when all men turned away from him, stood by his side and accepted from his lips the words of God. The first

The Women of Islam

in Islam! and hers the proud title for all the ages, Mother of the Believers!

Mohammed, though often spoken of as a camel-driver, belonged to the first family in Mecca, that of El Hashim, and his uncle Abu Talib was the hereditary Prince of Mecca and guardian of the Kaba. Being, however, poor in worldly goods, like many another scion of a noble house, he accepted as a very young man, from the wealthy widow Kadijah, the position of the leader of her caravan.

Just how long this lasted, we do not know, but sooner or later the friends of Kadijah persuaded her that she should not remain a widow, and she gave her hand to the young Mohammed, who at the time was twenty-six, she herself being forty years old.

A marriage *de convenance* in the beginning, but a real union of hearts as it proved. Six children were born to them, four daughters and two sons, the latter of whom

A Key to the Orient

died, to the Prophet's deep regret; but the daughters were cherished and prized, and Mohammed taught his countrymen to value their girls as they had never done before, for, as he said, "If you have sons, it is well; but if you have daughters only, it is well also." Through all the storms of his eventful life, Kadijah stood firm and true by the side of Mohammed; and in turn, though he might have had as many wives as he pleased, his heart never swerved from her, and he never in her life-time took another.

In later years, indeed, he took to himself seven wives; but even then the Mother of Believers was not forgotten, and Ayesha, his favorite of them all, averred that she was never jealous of any of his living wives, but only of the memory of Kadijah.

Of these seven wives, though all their names are known, but two have left footprints in history, — Ayesha and Mary.

The Women of Islam

Some of them were presents which the Prophet was more or less obliged to accept; and it is probable that the desire for a son, more than the fancy for a large harem, actuated the Prophet in taking to himself so many.

His desire, however, was not destined to be fulfilled. The only child ever born to Mohammed, except by Kadijah, was Ibrahim, the son of Mary. Great was the Prophet's joy, and that of his followers, at his birth, but a joy soon to be turned into sorrow, for after six months little Ibrahim died.

His death was accompanied by an eclipse of the sun, which the Arabs pronounced the result of the sad event. But Mohammed, who had never claimed to be more than a man, reproved them for their superstition, and nobly said that human events had no power over sun, moon, or stars, the lamps of God.

When Mohammed had established his

A Key to the Orient

religion in Arabia, he sent messengers to the rulers of all the surrounding countries to summon them to embrace Islam, and accept him as the Prophet of God. His messengers were received with laughter, but laughter that was soon to be turned into tears, when the summons was repeated by armies before their gates, and when their painted Saints could not save them from the sword of Islam.

The only one who returned a polite answer was the Governor of Egypt, and with it he sent, as a present to Mohammed, two beautiful young girls, the most beautiful of whom was Mary.

Mohammed took her to wife, and is said to have loved her, and had Ibrahim lived she might have become a power in Islam, but after his death her star seems to have set, and she fades out of history.

Ayesha was the daughter of Abu Bekr, a prominent citizen of Mecca, and one of the first and most ardent of the followers of

The Women of Islam

Mohammed. He it was who accompanied the Prophet in his second flight from Mecca, and was with him in the celebrated scene in the cave, where they were hiding from their persecutors who swarmed on the mountains. Overcome by the danger, Abu Bekr gave himself up for lost, saying, "We are but two against them all."

"Nay," said Mohammed, "we are three, for God is with us."

This adventure gained for Abu Bekr the name of the other one of the two, and it was in consequence of this, that being considered the nearest to the Prophet, he was chosen as his successor, and became the first of the Kalifs. Mohammed, after he became Lord of Arabia, married Ayesha, then only twelve years old, out of compliment to her father. She was a clever as well as a beautiful woman, and soon became his favorite, and exercised a great influence in Islam, both during his life-time and under the reign of her father.

A Key to the Orient

Ali, the husband of Mohammed's favorite daughter Fatima, and afterwards fourth Kalif, was always hostile to Ayesha, and constant trouble existed between them. He even accused her of being unfaithful to the Prophet, and appearances seemed to justify the accusation, but Mohammed would not doubt her; she remained with him always first, and he finally expired in her arms.

Of the daughters of Mohammed, Fatima is by far the most prominent. The wife of Ali and the mother of Hassan and Hosein, it is from her that all the descendants of the Prophet still flourishing in these days, claim their descent.

Another daughter, Rikayia, was so beautiful that Othman, himself the flower of the Arab youth, embraced Islam for her sake, and afterwards became the third Kalif; but the other two daughters have left no trace in history.

And now to the religious and social

The Women of Islam

position accorded by the Arabian Prophet to women. The general impression on this subject amongst us is very false, and no man has ever been so maligned and misrepresented as Mohammed.

The reason for this is not far to seek. Until the present century our information, if such it can be called, about Mohammed and his teachings was derived chiefly from the Greek priests,—the Greek priests, who were not only his enemies, but, as Lady Mary Montagu very justly remarks, "Undoubtably the greatest set of liars and scoundrels that the world has ever seen."

Mohammed was the champion of women, seeking in their case, as in all others, to do justice and right wrong.

To understand this we must look at the position of women in Arabia before his time. To begin with, it was quite a common custom among the Arabs to destroy their female infants, as the Chinese

A Key to the Orient

do to-day (they would not kill them, indeed, but they buried them alive).

Mohammed abolished this custom entirely, and taught that daughters were only second in value to sons.

Women had no rights of property, anything they had inherited became their husband's, and remained his should he divorce them, they being left penniless. The number of wives one might have was unlimited, and a man had the right to punish an unfaithful wife with death.

Mohammed changed all this, giving rights of property to women the same as to men, and obliging a man who divorced his wife to restore her dowry. The number of wives he limited to four, and took away from the husband the power of life and death.

He allowed men their female slaves, as had always been the custom, and as we see it in the Bible itself; but he made it a law that if there were children, they

The Women of Islam

should rank equally with the children of the wife or wives.

One of the commonest errors in regard to the teachings of Mohammed is that he denied immortality to women, and declared they had no souls. This is entirely false. Mohammed promised paradise to women on one condition, that of bearing children.

His own words in the Koran are as follows, " Women not being fitted by nature to direct in council nor to support the fatigues of war, God has not ordained that they shall govern or reform the world, but He has intrusted them with an office which is not less honorable, even that of multiplying the human race."

" And such as out of malice or laziness refuse to bear children fulfil not the duty of their vocation and rebel against the commands of God."

It is said that an old woman once asked Mohammed, if there would be any old women in heaven. " No," replied the

A Key to the Orient

Prophet, "before entering heaven they will all be made young."

Surely no promise can be better than this, and no woman can ask more than eternal youth in paradise.

The life of women in the East has always been one of seclusion, and this does not belong to any religion more than the others, but it is for many reasons a necessity.

Mohammed, indeed, ordained that the women should wear veils in public, but that had already been the custom in many parts of the East, though not among the Arabs, and is as strictly observed by the Asiatic Christians as by the women of Islam, to-day.

We are prone to imagine and believe that we owe our liberty to the Christian religion, but this is an entire mistake.

The teachings of Christ hardly touch on social institutions, and where the Apostles have laid down any rules, they

The Women of Islam

have been in accordance with the old régime, such as, that women should appear in the assemblies with their heads covered, and if they had anything to ask, should not speak in public, but ask their husbands at home.

The truth is that the Apostles were orientals, and that it never occurred to them to change any of their social regulations, change being entirely foreign to the oriental nature.

Had Christianity become the religion of Asia, instead of that of Europe, our present position would never have been attained, and the life of Christian women would have been just what the life of the oriental Christian women is to-day, practically the same as that of their Moslem neighbors.

But this was not to be: Christianity was destined to be the religion of progress, and, turning its back on Asia where it was not welcome, it spread its wings for

A Key to the Orient

Europe, where the old beliefs were dead and dying, and the time for a new faith had come.

The Roman Empire embraced Christianity, and Christianity adopted the social customs of the Roman Empire.

It is from the Romans that we get monogamy, which had always been their custom. As the Roman dominion had been some time established in Judea before the coming of Christ, it is most likely that this was practised by the Christians from the first, but a Jewish custom it certainly was not, till they too took it from the Romans.

And from the Romans comes our right to social intercourse with men, which had even been denied to respectable women by the Greeks, and all our marriage rites, our bridal veils, our bridesmaids, and our wedding rings, — the whole foundation of the position which we enjoy to-day.

The Women of Islam

Let no one suppose that I undervalue what woman gained through Christianity. I am speaking not of her spiritual elevation, but of her social position.

The worship of the Mother of Christ placed woman on a pedestal, and lit a halo round her head.

But among the Gothic and their kindred nations, the seclusion of the early Christian woman was that of a saint in its shrine, and it was not until the end of the dark ages, that with the return of Roman influences she resumed the position which she had held in the Roman Empire.

But to return to the women of the Orient, their life is one of seclusion and has been such throughout all Asia since the dawn of time.

Centuries have passed and made no difference. The pictures of oriental life and social customs which we find in the Arabian Nights of the time of Haroun-al-

A Key to the Orient

Raschid, the contemporary of Charlemagne, are just as true to-day. And still the same, are the glittering scenes of the Shah Namah, the great Persian epic poem, and still the history of Zal and Rudabe, the most famous of its legends, ranks first of oriental love-stories, though three thousand years old.

Woman in the Orient has always been a thing of beauty rather than of use, the partner of man's pleasures, not his toils.

Never has she been considered his equal, but she has been guarded as a treasure, never permitted to do anything for her own support, and shielded from all conflict with the outside world.

Much has been said and written about the degradation of this mode of life, principally by people quite ignorant of what they were talking about; but there are two sides to everything.

Undoubtably there have been in all ages domestic tragedies and scandals

The Women of Islam

occurring in harems, but have there been none in Christian countries, and are there none in our highly civilized and model homes to-day? and as our lights are greater than the Moslems, are we not more to blame?

In reality the lives of most oriental women are, if monotonous and dull according to our ideas, peaceful and happy according to their own, and absolutely devoid of most of the little worries and struggles which bring us wrinkles and gray hairs before our time.

To begin with, as the salvation of women depends on their being mothers, or at least endeavoring to fulfil their destiny, all girls are given in marriage as soon as they have reached the marriageable age, which varies with them according to latitude, from eleven or twelve to seventeen or eighteen. These marriages, which we regard as deplorable because the bride and bridegroom cannot know each

A Key to the Orient

other beforehand, and meet for the first time on their wedding night, are in reality quite as happy and as successful as our own.

In the first place, they are arranged by their respective mothers, who should know their children best, with regard to suitability of age, disposition, and social rank.

The bridegroom's mother also seeks beauty in her son's bride, and he, with that filial piety which is one of the strongest sentiments in the East, sees through her eyes and makes her taste his own.

But here the young girl has the advantage of sight over faith, for she may see the young man through her window lattices or on the street, he being always shown to her in this way, and if he does not please her fancy, it is rare that her inclination is forced.

They meet then on the wedding night, and both being very young, and having known no other youths or maidens, and

The Women of Islam

being therefore without rivals in each other's minds, it is natural that they should love each other.

Young people in the East rarely set up establishments of their own, but live either with the parents of the bridegroom or the bride.

The young wife then has no household cares, which are indeed considered unsuitable for young women. The harem is governed by her mother or mother-in-law, as it may be, and the whole duty of the bride consists in cultivating her beauty and trying to please her husband.

When she becomes a mother, she has fulfilled her destiny, her life is full, and her hopes of paradise secure.

Her days run calmly on, only broken by the rejoicings over successive babes, and by the excitement of other weddings in her family, and at last she is called to take the place of honor vacated by her mother or mother-in-law, and to rule the harem.

A Key to the Orient

The most beautiful thing in the oriental life is that the oriental husband looks for and finds his pleasures at home. There are no clubs in the Orient, no bar-rooms or saloons, and men cannot flirt with other men's wives, to the neglect of their own. There are not even operas or theatres. The outside world is the place for business, for education, diplomacy, law, and war; but the pleasures of life are all at home.

An oriental friend of mine once said to me, "With us a man must marry; how else can he spend his evenings if he has no home."

And he expressed the situation perfectly. The Oriental, be he of high or low degree, returns to his house in the afternoon, retires to his harem, and there spends the remainder of the day with his wife and the other women of his family, playing with his children and enjoying his home. If he be a rich man and the pos-

The Women of Islam

sessor of female slaves, they sing and dance before him and the ladies of the family, and add to the general amusement, according to their accomplishments.

As to the question of polygamy, which would certainly destroy domestic happiness (according to our ideas), I cannot believe that it has ever been a general custom.

My own experience of oriental life has been entirely in Egypt and Turkey. I have seen the inside of many homes in these two countries, from the palaces of the Pashas to the mud huts of the fellaheen, but never anywhere have I found more than one wife.

Lady Mary Montagu, who saw Turkey in its glory, makes the same assertion that "though the men are allowed four wives by their religion, it is a luxury in which they do not indulge themselves," and in all her visits in the harems, though she had found troops of female slaves, there was never but one wife.

A Key to the Orient

Still there are instances of a plurality of wives in both these countries, and I am told that in Arabia and Persia it is still the general custom.

Perhaps it is true, but I can only say that being a student of oriental literature myself, I have very seldom found the story, of no matter what age or country, in which more than one wife appears, and the most casual reader must have observed the same thing in the Arabian Nights.

My Turkish friends tell me that nowadays a man who likes variety in his marital relations takes his wives in succession, instead of all at once, divorcing one and marrying another, but only having one at a time.

This, they say, is less expensive and more agreeable; but in the days of their grandfathers, they add, the old customs were still adhered to and every great and rich man kept a large harem. I know indeed one noble Turkish family

The Women of Islam

whose paternal grandfather had six wives, four at a time, and whose maternal grandfather had a hundred and fifty women in his harem.

But the answer to the question is here: both these grandfathers were governors of provinces and Pashas of the first degree, and their revenues enabled them to keep up establishments which the general decrease in the wealth of the Turkish Empire will not permit to-day.

The Padishah of course, and the lesser sultans in his train, the rulers of Arabia and the Barbary States, have, as they always have had, large harems, and doubtless will have for all time to come.

But this proves nothing, for a large harem is something which (whether kept within the four walls of a Serail or allowed to roam the world at will) seems to belong to royalty.

The liberty and amusements of Moslem women vary in different countries.

A Key to the Orient

In Egypt their diversions are fewer and their liberty less than in Turkey, and in Persia and Arabia they are kept much more strictly still. In all oriental countries the great excitement and dissipation of the ladies are weddings, and these are indeed the only entertainments which they attend. Visiting and shopping in the bazaars are also among their diversions, but where the old régime prevails these are pleasures which are very much restricted.

In Cairo one meets women of the lower classes in the bazaars and walking on the streets, but very rarely ladies, either walking or driving, and then always accompanied by eunuchs; and the inference is, that, except for visits to their relatives, weddings, or very occasional shopping tours, they stay at home.

The Turkish ladies, on the contrary, lead a very gay life, and seem to be always on the go, walking, driving, visiting, or boating in caiques.

The Women of Islam

When one goes to visit an Egyptian harem, it is almost as unnecessary to ask if the ladies are at home as when visiting a convent, but in Constantinople it is better to send word of one's coming beforehand, if one does not go by special invitation.

Eunuchs are rare at present in Constantinople, or at least they are not much seen on the streets; and though no Turkish lady ever goes out alone, one sees them both walking and driving two or three together, or attended only by their female slaves.

The Egyptian and Persian veils are so thick and black that it is impossible to see anything but a woman's eyes, or to tell whether she is old or young. But the Turkish yashmak, which is made of a fine white silk gauze, not only does not hide, but heightens the beauty of the wearer, like a bridal veil.

All things are ordered for the best;

A Key to the Orient

though there are many handsome women in Egypt among the fellaheen and Abyssinian slaves, the lack of beauty among the ladies is very marked, and is all the more surprising as the husbands are, as a rule, very handsome men. And for this reason they are more interesting with, than they would be without, their thick black veils.

But in Turkey all the women are beautiful, or at least pleasing to the eye, and the yashmak is just what is needed to give the last touch to their charms.

Of course so much liberty and such thin veils would soon pervert the position of the Turkish women, but that though they are seen they are never known. One may feast his eyes on beauty, white skins, pink cheeks, red lips, and long black-velvet eyes, but one may never know who these sisters of the houris are. No Turk ever recognizes his wife, or any of his female relatives, in the

The Women of Islam

street, and for a man to ask him any question concerning them, or even to refer to the fact that they exist, would be the height of bad breeding and discourtesy.

No man is allowed to follow or even stare at a woman on the street, and yet human nature is the same here as elsewhere; where there is a will there is a way, and a friend of mine, a young Turkish Bey, has explained to me how lovematches are made even here.

The Turkish ladies are very fond of making picnics, which they do by going in their caiques in spring to " The sweet waters of Europe," an ideally beautiful stream at the head of the Golden Horn, and in summer to a smaller but equally beautiful and winding stream which flows into the Bosphorus, " The sweet waters of Asia."

Arrived at these places, which are assuredly two of the most beautiful spots in the world, the ladies sit together on one

A Key to the Orient

side of the stream, and the gentlemen on the other. They listen to open-air concerts, and regale themselves on coffee and sweets, and watch the gypsies dance. All very innocent apparently, but once in their caiques again on the serpentine curves of the little river, the boats pass close to each other, and (the words are the Bey's not my own) " The youths and maidens who have taken each other's fancy across the stream make signs to each other." Then seemingly without intention the lover follows the lady's boat, trying to learn from some one to whom belong the rowers, or where she will land. Perhaps his own oarsmen may recognize their fellows, and know in whose service they are, or it may take many afternoons of such meetings to unravel the mystery. But once known, unless indeed the lady be already married, the case becomes a simple one. The young man sends his mother, or some other female relative, to see the young

The Women of Islam

lady's mother, and propose for her, and then, if the affair can be arranged, which generally happens, the marriage takes place, and is as much of a love-match in its way as any of ours.

With regard to Moslem weddings, I would just say here for the benefit of oriental travellers that there are no regular invitations, but all ladies who choose are expected to attend, just as the friends of the family are expected at funerals with us.

On bright spring afternoons in Constantinople and Cairo, one often sees a stream of carriages full of ladies, of whose jewels and bright brocades and tinsel one catches glimpses, all hurrying in one direction. It is a wedding, and one has only to make one's dragoman find out where it is, provide one's self with a bouquet or other small present, and follow. Oriental hospitality never fails, and a foreign lady is always welcome.

In Arabia and Persia and further East,

A Key to the Orient

the old customs still exist in everything; but in Turkey, and to some extent in Egypt, people are divided into two parties, the advanced and the conservative.

It is not my purpose to speak of the men of these countries, but only of the women, and I have found that for them the difference in these two parties consists chiefly in three things, — the number of men they are allowed to see and know, their education and costume.

According to the laws of the Prophet, a man is only allowed to see the following number of women: His grandmother, mother, sister, foster-sister, wife, and daughters, and, of course, female slaves. This custom is still adhered to by the strict conservatives, but even with them I believe it is usual that a man should see his sisters-in-law and daughters-in-law when they live in his own house, and the usage is almost universal that a man should enjoy the society of his mother-in-law.

The Women of Islam

The advanced school admits all his "in-laws," and in Turkey the aunts, nieces, and cousins. It has always been the custom of the great men to assemble around them their poor relations, and to take them to live in their palaces, which, of course, means the addition of all the poor female relatives to the harem.

This of course adds to the gayety of the harem, by giving more companions to the ladies of the family; and it can be, and often is, managed that all the different men visit their own women without ever seeing those who do not belong to them.

But where the new régime allows all the cousins to meet and know each other, we have quite a new state of things. The ideal of the happy family is realized, and each house is a little world in itself, quite independent of the great world outside.

The education of oriental women has always been very simple. They are taught embroidery and music, and, if they have

A Key to the Orient

any voices, to sing, and sometimes to read the Koran.

Dancing is an art much cultivated, but never taught to ladies, only to slaves; and the daughter of Herodias is the only oriental lady on record who ever danced.

The advanced party, on the contrary, import French *bonnes* and governesses for their daughters, and have them taught to play on the piano, instead of on the old-time lute. The young ladies seem to learn French easily, and do so gladly in order to read French novels, having few books of their own, and the days of wandering story-tellers, who formerly added so much to their amusement, being, in Turkey at least, almost past.

The beautiful Turkish costume, so well described by Lady Mary Montagu and other writers, has now become a thing of the past; but, though much less effective, they still have in Turkey and Egypt a costume of their own. This consists in a

The Women of Islam

long robe made, as we should say, "princess," and either fitting tight to the figure, or drawn in at the waist with a girdle of silver or gold. Sometimes this gown has a long train, which adds to its grace, and it is always high neck and long sleeves, Mohammedan women considering *décolleté* dresses immodest even in the seclusion of their homes.

It is also considered immodest to go bare-headed, and only permitted in very young girls, who generally wear their hair in two long plaits. The Egyptian women wear long silk veils, very graceful, and much like the Spanish mantilla; and the Turkish women wear little turbans of white tulle or embroidered silk gauze, to which are added, on festive occasions, a profusion of jewels, and sometimes the turban is dispensed with altogether, and the head covered with jewels alone.

There is another costume which I have seen in Turkey, but never in Egypt, con-

A Key to the Orient

sisting of a skirt and square sack, such as were worn at the time of the marriage of the Princess of Wales. I have only seen it worn by slaves, and though then made of the brightest brocades, I found it devoid of all grace.

The ladies of the advanced party wear French costumes and corsets, retaining only their turban and gold-embroidered slippers. But on the street the yashmak and burnous are obligatory, and the costume of all is the same.

I will close this article with a few of my own experiences in Egypt and Turkey, selecting those which will be the most interesting and the best calculated to give a true glimpse of harem life in the East of to-day.

The Women of Islam

Part II

My first experience was humble but none the less interesting. Our dragoman at Luxor, Mahmoud, a clever and amusing Arab, encouraged by my interest in everything Moslem, confided in me his family history, and the fact that he was newly married to a beautiful young girl of thirteen who belonged to the best of Luxor, and was named Fatima.

When I expressed a wish to see the little bride, he was much flattered, and the next morning took me to his house, threading our way first through the loaded camels and donkeys in the square, for it was market day, and then through a maze of narrow crooked streets.

The house was two stories high, and built of mud bricks like most of the houses in Luxor. And a massive wooden gate admitted us into a little courtyard, which

A Key to the Orient

seemed to serve as a reception-room also. A tall handsome woman, wrapped in a red-and-green silk veil put on like a mantilla and falling to her feet, came forward and kissed my hand.

This was Mahmoud's brother's wife. She conducted me to one corner of the court, where two green-and-white straw chairs were placed on a Turkish rug, and as soon as I was seated brought me some coffee in a white-and-gold cup.

A few moments later the little bride appeared, and after kissing my hand seated herself in the other chair. Mahmoud and his sister-in-law sat down on the ground, and we all began an animated conversation in English and Arabic, Mahmoud acting as interpreter.

Fatima was as pretty a little creature as I have ever seen, and did not look older than a girl of thirteen looks in America.

Her skin was like the richest cream, and she had the red lips, pink cheeks, and long

The Women of Islam

black eyes inseparable from the oriental ideal of beauty.

She was very bright and gay, constantly looked at Mahmoud, and laughed and seemed perfectly happy.

Her costume would have been a surprise to any one who did not know the East, and who remembered that her husband earned but six shillings a day. Her dress was ruby-red silk, and her veil of red-and-green silk gauze, a massive gold necklace like a row of medallions hung round her neck, and four heavy gold earrings hung two in each ear. Immense silver bracelets clasped her wrists, and her fingers were loaded with rings.

A woman of her position in America would have been dressed in cotton, and immersed in household work; but work was evidently unknown to Fatima.

I asked Mahmoud how she spent her time.

"Oh," he said, " she sits here and talks

to my female relatives, and her mother comes to see her every morning and every evening."

I asked him if she never went out.

"Oh, yes," he said, "sometimes at night with my mother or sister, but not to her father's house; she will not go there till we have been married twelve months. She stays always here because she is so young, and that she may get accustomed to my family, but when twelve months are out, she will go home and stay a few days with her father and mother. And before she goes, I must give her a present that she go away content; and before she returns, they must give her one that she come back happy."

We talked on with a flowing interchange of compliments, as always in an oriental conversation. Fatima begged me to come back and see her again if I ever returned to Luxor, and I gave her a pin in the shape of a lantern as a souvenir.

The Women of Islam

At this she was much delighted, and vowed that she would never forget me, and that she would send me a present in return.

Both she and her sister-in-law kissed my hands many times at parting, and the same afternoon I received a quantity of blue beads and several small blue mummies such as one finds in the tombs, from my little friend Fatima.

To cross the Mediterranean at a bound, and give a glimpse of modern Turkey, I will tell of two visits in Constantinople, one in the house of an advanced Pasha, and the other in that of a very conservative Bey, which will show that the conflicting accounts that one hears on this subject may be equally true.

Arrived in the house of the Pasha, I was met in the Salamlik (the men's part of the house) by the Pasha's eldest son, who conducted me down a long passage into the harem.

This, as in most great establishments,

A Key to the Orient

was in a separate house with a garden of its own and built on the very edge of the Bosphorus, so that but for the lattices one might fish directly out of the windows.

The lower floor of the house was arranged as most large Turkish houses are, all the rooms opening from a round central hall supported on pillars, with two fine staircases, one at each side.

The oriental staircase is invariable, and differs from ours in that it starts with two flights from the ground and continues from the landing in one. And I have even seen some in the palaces which make a double turn in the air.

We ascended to the second floor, which was arranged in the same way, and there we were met by two ladies, both young and beautiful, to whom the Bey introduced me, his wife and sister.

The ladies conducted me into a salon which was a great disappointment to me, being entirely European. The furniture

The Women of Islam

was Louis Fourteenth (of which style the orientals seem particularly fond), covered in green-and-gold brocade. The walls were green and gold, and, alas! an Axminster carpet covered the floor. But for the window lattices we might have been in Germany or France.

The wife of the Bey was an Austrian by birth whom he had met and married in Vienna, and who had renounced the world and adopted the Moslem mode of life for his sake.

She was very pretty, and seemed perfectly satisfied. Her religion was the only thing which she had retained; but her two pretty little children, a girl and a boy, were being reared in the faith of Islam.

Both she and her sister-in-law were dressed in the Paris fashions, another disappointment to me; but the sister was an ideal oriental beauty whom no chiffons could change or spoil, a real princess of the Arabian Nights.

A Key to the Orient

She spoke French to me, and her voice was like music. Never have I seen anywhere a more lovely or attractive young girl.

The Bey had left us, and the ladies entertained me by showing me photograph albums, and asking me about my travels (which seemed to interest them very much), and also many questions about America.

I had been invited to lunch, and thought of course to remain with the ladies; but no, the Bey reappeared and, saying lunch was served, took me back to the Salamlik, where my husband was waiting for me, and we three sat down to lunch in a handsome European dining-room. The room was occidental indeed, but the lunch was entirely oriental, — innumerable courses, and everything delicious, from the soup to the pilaf and sweets.

Oriental cooking is always good, but the Turkish cooking surpasses all others, and

The Women of Islam

distances the French. After lunch I returned to the harem and took my leave of the ladies, and then our host showed us his garden, and took us in his caique to that most beautiful spot, "The sweet waters of Asia."

Quite different was my visit to the house of a Bey who is one of the most conservative men in Constantinople, and where I had the pleasure of finding everything according to the old régime.

To this house I was conducted by the Bey's nephew, another young Bey whom I had known in Vienna.

The house was in the middle of Stamboul. Wooden and unpretentious outside, but the moment the street-door was opened we found ourselves in a marble hall, and a number of jet-black eunuchs conducted us up a marble staircase to the second floor, which in this case was the harem.

Here we were ushered into a room

A Key to the Orient

where sat the Bey, a fine-looking old man with a white beard and bright black eyes, wearing a fez, of course, and a long fur-lined gown.

He rose at our entrance, shook hands with my husband and bowed to me, bidding us welcome in Turkish; for he spoke no other language, and I noticed with interest that he held and fingered a rosary of enamel and pearls.

The room was half Turkish, half European, and around the walls were a quantity of rare and beautiful clocks on brackets, of which, and especially of watches, I was told the Bey was a great collector and connoisseur.

In a few moments a eunuch reappeared to say that the ladies were waiting, and, accompanied by the young Bey, I walked down a corridor into what was evidently the reception-room of the harem.

This was a large room frescoed in different colors. A row of yellow-satin

The Women of Islam

sofas and chairs were arranged around the walls, a glass chandelier full of candles in bell-glasses hung from the middle of the ceiling, and under it stood a superb brass brazier on a large brass tray.

The wife of the Bey advanced to meet me, a handsome woman of middle age, with splendid black eyes. To my delight she wore a Turkish dress of yellow satin, with a sweeping train, and a little turban of embroidered gauze. An Indian scarf hung over her shoulders, and her diamonds, of immense size and brilliancy, fairly dazzled the sight.

She greeted me with great cordiality in Turkish, and presented me to two ladies who had been invited to meet me, one a woman of thirty-five or so, in semi-European dress, and the other a girl of fifteen with her hair in long plaits and wearing a pelisse of crimson velvet embroidered in pearls.

All the ladies shook hands with me, and,

A Key to the Orient

according to the Turkish custom, they tried to get their hands lower than mine, to show in what honor they held me. Politeness forced me to follow suit, and the result was we shook hands on the floor.

We all sat down, and immediately four slaves entered the room, bearing bon-bons and coffee, all but one, who wore the Greek costume and seated herself on the floor, while the others remained standing.

My friend, the Bey, explained to me that she had been the wet nurse of the eldest son, and in consequence ranked second only to the ladies of the family.

The bon-bons were first handed round, — delicious Turkish bon-bons in dishes of silver filigree, — and then the coffee in cups of egg-shell porcelain fitting into outside cups of gold, the whole service resting on a round silver-gilt tray. And last of all came pink sherbet in large glasses, the usual order observed everywhere.

The Women of Islam

The slaves interested me extremely. They were all young women, one Circassian and two negresses, all dressed in white tulle turbans and skirts, and jackets of brilliant brocade, — one pink, one lilac, and one olive-green.

The ladies spoke nothing but Turkish, but that made no difference; they talked to me with the greatest volubility, and the Bey acted as interpreter.

Knowing a little Turkish myself, I said what I could, and the ladies were delighted with my efforts, and clapped their hands and laughed, and begged me to say something more, until my vocabulary was entirely exhausted.

A great many compliments were exchanged between us, and the ladies talked of their family affairs just as women do in America.

The wife of the Bey related with great glee that she had gone out in a white veil for the first time in her life the day be-

A Key to the Orient

fore. And her cousin told us in confidence that her daughter, a bride of fifteen, was not permitted by her husband to wear anything but a dark-figured veil, and added that her son-in-law was very jealous.

They were all very merry and bright, and made me feel very much at home. I lingered as long as I thought correct, though they begged me to stay, and we parted with vows of eternal friendship.

To close this article with an account of what is at the present day the most oriental of all oriental things, I will tell of a wedding, and a wedding on the grandest scale, which I was fortunate enough to witness in Cairo.

This was the wedding of a certain Mohammed Bey to the daughter of Hassan Pasha, both representatives of the highest Egyptian aristocracy. And while the oriental ideas of friendship have forbidden me to mention the names of my Turkish friends, while relating what I saw in their

The Women of Islam

homes, I feel at liberty to give all the names here, because all great weddings are alike, and rank less as private than as official events.

An oriental wedding always takes place at the house in which the young couple are to reside, but the evening before the contract is signed at the home of the bride.

All the male friends and relatives on both sides assemble, and there is what we would call a stag party. The contract is signed by the bridegroom and the fathers or guardians on both sides, and last of all the bride is called, and comes veiled to the door of the harem, where she is met by the priest. He asks her if she is willing to marry the young man, she says yes, and the ceremony is complete. Every one then separates, and the real wedding takes place the next day as follows.

I arrived at the palace of Achmet Pasha, the brother of Mohammed Bey, at five

A Key to the Orient

o'clock in the afternoon, as all the other guests were assembling. The street for a square on each side was spanned with arches hung with colored lanterns, gold and silver balls, and Turkish flags, and the gateway was garlanded with crimson flowers.

A glimpse into the courtyard showed me the Pasha surrounded by his friends seated on innumerable divans, drinking coffee and smoking cigarettes.

But only a glimpse; for a jet-black eunuch hurried me through a side door, and up a flight of stairs into the harem, where I found myself at once in the Arabian Nights.

The palace was of immense size, and built around a courtyard three rooms deep, the inside suite having windows on the courtyard, and the outside on the street, the middle rooms being lit by skylights. All the rooms were very much alike, furnished with divans and curtains of

The Women of Islam

different-colored brocade. In some of them were large canopied Turkish beds, and in some French consoles and tables, and almost every room boasted a crystal chandelier. Opening as they did out of each other, these brilliant and endless rooms gave one the feeling of the palace of a dream.

Perhaps two hundred women or more were walking about or sitting on divans,— the ladies of Cairo and their slaves, Egyptians, Circassians, and Abyssinians.

They were all in Egyptian costumes of the most gorgeous materials, brilliant pinks and lilacs, sky-blues and ruby-reds, many of them brocaded in gold flowers, and nearly all belted in at the waist with girdles of flexible gold.

The slaves wore dresses as rich as the ladies, but their necklaces, bracelets, and earrings were in most cases only of gold, while the ladies, one and all, fairly glittered with diamonds.

A Key to the Orient

The jewels indeed were surprising. Every lady wore a diamond necklace, and most of them long diamond earrings, diamond bracelets, diamond chatelaines, and medallions of diamonds holding their husbands' pictures pinned over their hearts.

Some of the ladies wore Turkish turbans under which jewels glittered like stars through a mist. One had a number of diamond humming-birds nestling in her hair, but the majority wore diamond tiaras as large as the usual royal coronet.

Some few of the slaves wore diamonds also, and I began to realize that Egypt is still the richest country in the world.

The absence of other jewels surprised me, though there were some fine pearls and emeralds. And I also wondered why there were only the four colors I have mentioned. Green I knew was forbidden by the strict letter of the Koran, being the Prophet's color, but I could not understand the absence of yellow.

The Women of Islam

After I had feasted a few moments on this fairy scene, a large negress conducted me into a room where the wedding presents were displayed in glass cabinets against the walls. These consisted of articles of gold and silver plate and bottles of perfume. From there I went into the *salon d'honneur* where the bride was to be received. This was a large room somewhat in European style, with furniture of heavy carved rose-wood ranged around the walls, a crimson carpet, and curtains and portières of crimson-and-gold brocade.

At one side was a dais raised three steps, and covered with crimson satin, on which stood two massive Louis the Fourteenth gilt chairs covered with crimson-and-gold brocade, and over them, supported on slender gilt columns, a splendid canopy with sweeping curtains of crimson satin fringed with gold.

Nor was this all, but from the top of each column hung a skein of gold wire as

A Key to the Orient

thick as a man's arm, which reached the floor.

A sudden cry arose that the bride was coming, and all the women rushed to the windows, I among the rest, and just in time to see what might have been Cinderella's chariot stop the way, — a gilded coach of nondescript design, over the roof of which, as is their custom, was thrown a rich white Indian shawl.

The bride had alighted, and was coming up the stairs; and, running out into the ante-chamber, I saw her enter her new home, entirely covered with a golden veil, and surrounded by twelve jet-black eunuchs, all throwing silver money in the air.

They passed into the *salon d'honneur*, and the moment afterwards the slaves went down on their hands and knees, tumbling over each other to get the money. The ladies had to jump up on the divans to save themselves from being thrown

The Women of Islam

down, and the floor was a scrambling mass of satin and brocade.

When I could make my way back to the *salon d'honneur*, I found the bride already unveiled and seated in one of the chairs on the dais. An Abyssinian slave sat at her feet and fanned her, and the admiring throng of women crowded on every side.

The bride was, as I was informed, seventeen, rather old for an Egyptian bride. I wish I could relate that she was beautiful; but though she had the splendid black eyes of her race, and luxuriant black hair, I can describe her best by saying that she was twice too stout.

Her dress was of the richest material of the East, a pigeon's-blood Mecca silk brocaded with gold flowers. A gold belt encircled her waist, and on her head she wore a white tulle turban from which two skeins of gold wire, like the skeins on the canopy, hung over her shoulders and down

A Key to the Orient

to the ground. Her turban was fairly ablaze with diamonds, and her bosom was covered with a mass of diamond flowers.

Her slave was dressed in brocade of brilliant lilac; and the color and glitter of the whole picture may be better imagined than described.

The bride remained perfectly silent, and no one spoke to her. Her position, everything depending on her as it did, seemed to me like that of the man at the wheel.

After a few moments more, she arose and descended from the dais. Her female relatives surrounded her, and led her out of the salon and into a private room. The ladies dispersed themselves again through the apartments, and I followed, with another American lady who was present, to see all that could be seen.

The ladies seated themselves on the divans, and little negresses carried round cigarettes in little baskets of gold and silver tinsel, and coffee in egg-shell cups.

The Women of Islam

Every lady sat with her own slave beside her, and I could not but remark that all the beauty was among the slaves.

The Egyptian ladies are, as I have said before, not beautiful. But the Abyssinians, although as dark as our mulattoes, are a very handsome race.

In Africa one entirely loses the idea that brown or even black skins mean negro blood. The Abyssinians have very noble features, and hair like waved black silk; and the Soudanese, though almost black, are the most beautiful and graceful creatures I have ever seen.

There were also a number of Circassian women present, easily told by their pink-and-white complexions, and their golden or auburn hair. These might have been beautiful, but that they were all blacked so heavily around their eyes that they seemed to be wearing spectacles, and that their natural eyebrows were shaved and replaced by streaks of black paint half an inch broad.

A Key to the Orient

This is an ancient Persian custom, and I cannot tell why it is practised in Egypt; nor have I seen it elsewhere.

The palm of beauty rested with the Abyssinians, and they seemed to be the brightest as well; for they talked incessantly, and kept the other women laughing.

In one of the central rooms a band of female musicians sat on the floor playing on inlaid tambourines and lutes, and one on a bottle drum. And musicians, instruments, and the wild melody they were playing, all carried one back to the days of Haroun-al-Raschid.

The eunuchs walked about joking with the women, with that familiarity which they are always allowed. The air was sweet with ottar of roses and musk, and I felt myself indeed in the heart of the East.

Half the women spent their time in the inner rooms sitting on the window-sills, and looking down into the court. I

The Women of Islam

looked also, at the instigation of an Egyptian friend, and found it a brilliant scene, though not so interesting as the one in the harem.

The whole courtyard was roofed in with bunting of the brightest colors, and a forest of glass chandeliers hung (from nothing, apparently.) The pillars were twined with bunting, and the innumerable divans spread with rugs; and in the midst of all the glitter and color the Pasha and the bridegroom, his brother, were making merry with their friends.

The window lattice of course protected the women from sight; but their enjoyment of the view seemed endless, for, from afternoon until midnight, the window-seats were always full.

The lady of the house, Madame Achmet Pasha, now approached me most graciously, not having had time before; and though she only spoke Arabic, there was no misunderstanding of her welcome.

A Key to the Orient

She was a handsome woman, a Circassian. I was surprised to find her alone of the women in a somewhat European dress of black satin with yellow stripes. But I was informed that on these occasions it is not etiquette for the hostess to appear *en grande toilette*, it being supposed that she is too busy attending to the comfort of her guests to have had time to dress herself.

The banquet now came next in order. But being told that it would be served in the old style, all the women eating out of the dishes with their fingers, and etiquette obliging one to partake of every course, I excused myself and left, promising to return in the evening.

I returned at nine o'clock, and was received by the mother of the bride (a most amiable woman dressed in rose-colored brocade), who took me into the bridal chamber and explained everything to me in Arabic.

This room adjourned the *salon d'honneur*

The Women of Islam

from which it was separated by portières. It was all yellow,—curtains, portières, and divans of yellow brocade; and at one side stood the most beautiful bed I have ever seen.

A Turkish bed,—four slender gilded columns supporting a canopy from which hung white-satin curtains fringed with gold; three long flat white-satin pillows, edged with gold embroidery, were piled at one end, and the rest of the bed was covered by a magnificent white-satin spread embroidered all over in gold.

Two steps, covered with white satin and fringed with gold, led up to this regal couch, and even the top sheet was embroidered in gold. And over all was thrown a white-silk gauze as fine as a spider's web, and embroidered all in white, with a wonderful fairy embroidery.

The days of Haroun-al-Raschid are over; but, thank Heaven, the East still keeps its splendors!

A Key to the Orient

On a table beside the bed were two large cases of crimson velvet embroidered in gold, some silver-backed brushes, a cigarette case, and match-box of gold, and a set of diamond studs and sleeve buttons.

I now returned to the other ladies, and found that many of them had changed their dresses; but there were no new colors, only paler and less effective shades.

They were all very cordial and friendly, and very anxious to talk to me. Two or three of them spoke French, and the bride's sister, an attractive young girl of fifteen, among the rest. And I found one who even spoke English, the only English-speaking oriental woman I have ever known.

She and I immediately became friends, and she presented to me her mother, a handsome old lady glittering with jewels, and her two daughters, girls of ten and twelve, with luxuriant curling ringlets of

The Women of Islam

light brown hair, most unusual in the East, as pretty as wax dolls, and whose bright pink dresses made them look like roses.

The women who could speak no foreign tongue talked to me in Arabic, and their tones and gestures were so expressive that I managed to catch a good deal of their meaning. I answered them in French, and we got along very happily. Women must talk, and I do not believe there is any difference of language so great as to render conversation between them absolutely impossible.

A very pretty Abyssinian woman, dressed in sky-blue brocade and sparkling with diamonds, came to me and said that she would go with me to America.

I told her I would take her with pleasure, and she turned to a number of other women and told them what she was going to do in America. The bride's sister, who sat beside me, translated what she said, and I must own that her ideas of our

A Key to the Orient

manners and morals were anything but flattering, so much so that my little friend at last apologized for her, and stopped translating.

But all other diversion was now put to an end by the announcement that the bride would now make her second *entrée*.

I went into the *salon d'honneur* and saw her enter, led by her sister and another young girl, walking with feigned reluctance, and apparently dragged along by her bridesmaids.

The sister was dressed in light blue, and the other young girl in white brocade, and loaded with emeralds and diamonds. She, the other, was the daughter of a great Pasha, and was soon to be married to the brother of my English-speaking friend.

The bride now wore a dress of white satin, brocaded with silver flowers; but her turban, her skeins of gold wire, and her diamonds remained unchanged.

Again she was lead to the seat on the

The Women of Islam

dais, and again the women gathered round her, and admired her to their hearts' content.

She remained as silent as before, and at the end of ten minutes or more she descended from her throne and sought refuge again in her private room.

We returned to the central apartments, and sat around on the divans. The female musicians whom I had seen in the afternoon reappeared and seated themselves on the floor, and with them came the nautch dancers.

Since the Chicago Fair so much has been written and said against the nautch dance that I will express no opinion on the subject, though being familiar with it in the East I might perhaps do so more intelligently than some of those who have condemned it so clamorously here.

I will make one remark and one only. The object of the nautch dance is to excite the senses. In Europe and America

A Key to the Orient

people at festive gatherings make themselves merry with a glass or two of champagne. Mohammed has forbidden wine, but he has not forbidden his followers to be merry. The nautch dance is the champagne of the Orient!

The costumes of the dancers on this occasion would have satisfied the severest critic, being just like those of the ladies, except without trains. Their hair, unlike the ladies', hung down in long plaits, and they wore round velvet caps embroidered in gold and pearls.

Coffee was brought to us again as we looked on, and the manner of serving it is worthy of note.

A negress carried a silver brazier, hanging like a censer by three chains, in which a superb coffee-pot rested on the coals. A second negress bore a round waiter with the cups, and a third served the coffee and handed it around.

The cups were like egg-shells, and at

The Women of Islam

the bottom of each under the coffee was a drop of ottar of rose.

The evening wore on, and at length we were informed by the watchers at the inside windows that the bridegroom had left the house with his especial friends to make his visit to the Mosque.

Perhaps half an hour more, and then a shouting and commotion in the streets, as in the Bible, " A cry arose at midnight, the bridegroom cometh !"

We all rushed to the windows, and looking down saw the procession coming along under the arches of colored lanterns and gold and silver balls, — twelve servants, all in white, each carrying a candle in a bell-glass, and walking in their midst a handsome young man of twenty one or two, Mohammed Bey.

A long string of young men, his friends, followed two and two, and slowly they all filed under the flower-hung gateway, and were lost to our view.

A Key to the Orient

The Egyptian ladies now began to wrap themselves in their burnouses and veils, and depart. The bridegroom was coming and they must not be seen, but my American friend and myself were invited to stay and witness the closing scene.

In company with the bride's mother and some of the house slaves, we stood in the doorway between the *salon d'honneur* and the bridal chamber, the heavy curtains half-hiding us from view.

The wife of Achmet Pasha entered the room, and stood before one of the windows, with three of her slaves behind her, and then came the bride, still in her white dress and covered from head to foot with her golden veil.

A prayer-rug of crimson velvet embroidered in gold was spread beside her, and behind her stood three of her slaves, all veiled in white. I confess that it was one of the most exciting moments of my life.

The Women of Islam

Footsteps were heard outside, and surrounded by twelve eunuchs, each with a candle in a bell-glass, Mohammed Bey entered the room.

He seemed embarrassed, and glancing at us behind the curtains stood still, but one of the eunuchs took him by the arm and led him to the praying-rug.

There he turned towards Mecca, dropped on his knees, and uttering a prayer touched the ground with his forehead three times.

Then rising, he took the bride's veil by the hem and lifted it slowly, slowly, and when the diamonds on her breast were in full sight her slaves seized it from behind and pulled it off, and she stood revealed in all her splendor.

Mohammed Bey clasped his hands in delight, and then turning to his sister-in-law uttered some words in Arabic, evidently expressive of joy. Then turning back again he gave his bride a medallion

A Key to the Orient

of diamonds, for which she made a place above her heart.

(It is an unwritten law in Islam that when a man sees his bride, his first act must be to give her a present.)

And then Mohammed Bey hesitated, but his sister encouraged him with a few words, and taking his bride by the hand he led her up on the dais, and they seated themselves on the two gilt chairs under the canopy.

The moment had come when these two thus mated for life were to make each other's acquaintance, but for us the spectacle was over. Madame Achmet Pasha rushed suddenly down upon us like a hawk on a brood of chickens, and pushed us all out of the room.

The crimson and gold portières were drawn behind us, and the Arabian Nights entertainment was at an end.

Oriental Slavery

ORIENTAL SLAVERY

WRITTEN IN 1892

READING the other day an account of the horrors of slavery in Morocco, I laughed at this new "bogie," as every one who knows the Orient and the oriental policy of England must.

The British lion loves to masquerade in the Crusader's mantle, and never sets out to seek his prey unarmed with a pious excuse.

The old Romans went out to conquer; but the English have no such intent, they go out only to spread freedom and Christianity — with the sword.

England wants Morocco, therefore this sudden outcry about Moorish slavery. When England has taken Morocco, Moorish slavery will be heard of no more.

A Key to the Orient

India, Burmah, Ceylon, and Egypt are full of slaves. And let it not be forgotten that General Gordon's first official act on his arrival in Khartoum was to re-establish, by edict of the Queen, the slave trade which had been abolished by the Khedive Ishmail. Nor can we blame him. Gordon knew the East and acted from necessity. I only blame that policy which talks one way and acts another. Let England conquer all she pleases, but let her have the courage of her actions, and not seek to humbug her own subjects and the rest of the world.

Many people speak of oriental slavery as of other things which they know nothing about. I know the East. Its religions, its history, and its literature have been with me almost a passion, and what its life is I have seen for myself. Its laws, customs, and social institutions are not and cannot be like ours. Who speaks of abolishing slavery in Mohammedan

Oriental Slavery

countries talks of something that he does not understand. Slavery, with them of the mildest and most patriarchal type, is almost a necessity of life, and more, it is a religious institution for which all the rules are laid down in the Koran.

To begin with men slaves. They are generally bought as boys from dealers or their own parents, and are carefully trained and taught whatever work, mental or manual, they are intended to perform.

Slavery in a Mohammedan country is no disgrace, nor does it debar a man from any career. Young white slaves are sometimes brought up as husbands for their master's daughters, and inherit their share of his wealth. Slaves who show intelligence and talent are often freed by their masters, after being carefully educated, and obtain through their influence official and sometimes very important positions. Talent has always found its recognition in the East, and, from the

A Key to the Orient

earliest times of Moslem history, slaves have risen to be generals, Pashas, governors of provinces, and even grand Viziers.

Before speaking of the slavery of women, we must consider the position of woman in the East, a most important point and one which the old maids of Exeter Hall, and many other good people, entirely forget.

Mohammed was the champion of women. He restricted the number of wives to four, gave women rights of property, obliged a man who divorced his wife to restore her dowry, and taught parents to be glad and proud of daughters as well as of sons.

No woman works for her living in the East. The poorest Mohammedan who would allow his wife, mother, daughter, or sister to go and work in another man's house would be disgraced. With them men only are the bread-winners, and without women slaves there would be no

Oriental Slavery

women servants of any kind, and this for another reason also, all oriental girls are married as soon as they reach the marriageable age,— a custom which insures peace and quiet, as much of the trouble in this world is made by single women (for the sole reason that they have nothing else to do).

The only exceptions to this rule are those unfortunates who are brought up as dancing and singing girls. They, however, are very few in number as compared with the immoral class in Christian countries. All other women marry, and old maids are unknown.

And now let us look at the real condition of the female slaves. In former times, there was a *commerce de luxe* in baby girls, who were prized for their beauty, and brought up in the harems with as much care as their master's daughters. Now they are generally bought as they are budding into womanhood, not in the

A Key to the Orient

slave-market as in olden times, but privately, from dealers to whom they have been sold by their parents, Circassia and Abyssinia being the great sources of supply. A female slave is more for ornament than use; her work consists in waiting on the ladies of the master's family, and keeping in order the apartments of the harem, all real work, such as cooking and washing, being done by the men.

When one pays a visit in a harem, all the slaves are brought in to serve the coffee and bon-bons, and remain standing about the room, silent and graceful, dressed in satin and brocade, bright with gold and silver ornaments, and sometimes glittering with jewels. They go out walking and driving with their mistresses, and are taken to weddings, which are almost the only entertainments in the East. An easy life compared with that of an English or American shop or factory girl, teacher, or sewing woman.

Oriental Slavery

And yet it is from this life that so many good people (ignorant and intolerant of all customs but their own) are so eager to rescue them — and for what? For what? — for since there is no work which women can do in the East, freedom to the slave means the choice between a life of shame and starvation on the streets.

As one of the many examples that may be given of the harm which is done by good people meddling in things they know nothing about, I will relate the following, which occurred in Egypt in the beginning of the English occupation, and which I have from an English officer who took part in the affair.

Information was received that five Abyssinian girls who had been ordered for the harem of a Pasha in Cairo were coming down the Nile in a *dahabiyeh*, and, in the language of Exeter Hall, a gun-boat was sent out to " rescue the unhappy girls

A Key to the Orient

from slavery," which in their case was to mean a transition from the mud huts of Abyssinia and an almost savage existence, to the luxury and splendor of a Cairene Palace, and a life of silks and jewels, bon-bons and perfumes.

The suspected boat soon appeared on the river, and, when summoned, refused to halt, whereupon the gun-boat fired a shot through her bows.

Brought to in this manner, she was boarded by the English, who found the girls below; but there were only four to rescue, for one had been killed by the English cannon-ball, — *her gift* from the good anti-slavists. The other four girls were taken down to Cairo, and there set at liberty, turned loose in the streets, speaking nothing but their own language, knowing nothing but the life of their distant home, young, children in years, and beautiful, and free! — free to choose between starvation and a life of shame.

Oriental Slavery

Oh, precious boon of liberty! Oh, excellent Exeter Hall!

The officer who told me this concluded by saying that it was the dirtiest piece of business in which he had ever been forced to take part, and that rather than engage in such another he would leave the service.

In former times, and still to some extent, the great men of the empire used to give slaves out of their own harems to their followers as presents and rewards. This was a high honor for the recipient. The slave became his wife, and, if he had other wives, took the first place. At present the usual custom is as follows: a Pasha or Bey or rich Effendi gives a slave her liberty after she has belonged to him three or four years. The woman then remains in his harem two or three years more, free, but leading the same life, clothed and fed and taken care of as before. At the end of that time the

A Key to the Orient

master finds her a suitable husband and gives her her dowry, the amount of which is regulated by custom. Afterwards, should her husband divorce her, she returns to her master's house, and in any case remains more or less a pensioner and dependent of his family, and his house remains to her a home. Some women remain always, from choice, in their master's harems. Those who have been wet nurses to their master's children are never given away; they are held in high honor and affection, waited upon by the other slaves, and ranked next to the ladies of the family.

One reads romantic tales of faithless odalisques sewn up in sacks and thrown into the sea; and in other times such things no doubt occurred, but these days are as much past as the days of witch burning in New England; and at least we must admit that the Mohammedans always take the most painless way of

Oriental Slavery

putting people to death, which is more than can be said of the Yankees.

And now let us look at female slavery from the point of morality.

Mohammed founded his religion on the Old Testament, which undeniably gives a slave to her master, as Abraham and Hagar, Jacob, Zilpah and Bilhah. To touch or even look at another man's wife is a sin for a Moslem, but a slave belongs to her master.

In the words of the Koran, "Take of what your right hands possess."

A Mohammedan is responsible for every child that is born in his house. If, therefore, a slave has a child by her master, the child ranks equal with the children of the wife or wives.

The Sultan never marries. All the women in the royal harem are slaves,—Circassians, Persians, Greeks, and negresses. Every woman who becomes a mother is called a Sultana, and her chil-

A Key to the Orient

dren are the Imperial Princes and Princesses. The real Queen is the Sultan's mother, who takes precedence of every one else, and bears the title of Sultana Validé. This lady is as much a necessity in her way as the Sultan in his. Therefore, if the Commander of the Faithful have no mother of his own, he must adopt one, to give a head to his harem.

When the present Sultan, Abdul Hamid, came to the throne, his own mother being dead, he adopted the mother of his predecessor, Abdul Aziz. A strange freak of fortune this! Through all the storms that shook the empire to its base, through the disasters of the war, the murder of her son, the death or exile of his ministers, this woman alone has remained, is Sultana Validé still. Like all her predecessors, once a slave, now first lady of the Ottoman Empire!

The Missionaries

THE MISSIONARIES

AS THEY APPEAR TO THE HEATHEN

NOW that the question has been raised in England, that the foreign missionaries are not fulfilling their mission,— and in some cases they are doing more harm than good,— a few words may be said on the subject here, also in the belief that it is always best that the truth should be told.

In the first place, I have no intent to attack the missionaries, but merely to show that they should be judged by their life and work abroad, rather than by our own imagination.

One hears of drunken and profligate missionaries, teaching the heathen the vices of our world, rather than the virtues of Christianity. Some such there are no

A Key to the Orient

doubt, and more who are ignorant or unfitted for their work; but most of them are good people, and doing good. But they are not doing what they have been sent to do, and what the good people at home are paying for.

They are teaching the natives English and something of the laws of sanitation and hygiene. The female missionaries are going into the harems and teaching some of the young girls to read and write, to sew and amuse themselves with fancy work. And where they are possessed of medical knowledge, they are curing little ailments, and sometimes even serious ones. And in Egypt and Syria especially they do an immense amount of good in saving eyes from the scourge of ophthalmia.

But they are not making converts to Christianity.

We are apt to speak of the heathen with utter indiscrimination.

The Missionaries

The learned Brahman, the Moslem, the Parsi, the Malay, and the African cannibal are all one to us. And we sing of them in our happy self-confidence and superiority as calling us from lands "Where every prospect pleases and only man is vile," "From Greenland's icy mountains to India's coral strand," to come and "Deliver their souls from error's chain."

In reality, however, there is all the difference in the world between the savage, bowing in simple ignorance before his "fetish" of wood or stone, and the devotee of a religion as firmly established and older than our own. And in point of fact, neither class of heathen is calling us, and when we go to convert them they decline our services with or without thanks, being as firmly convinced as ourselves that their religion is the best.

My own experience of missionaries has been entirely in Mohammedan countries,

A Key to the Orient

and any one who knows anything of Islam knows (perhaps from the very fact that their religion is founded upon ours) that it is impossible to convert a Moslem to Christianity.

The missionaries, being generally men and women of intelligence, soon realize this for themselves, and devote themselves to other good works, such as have been already mentioned. In Egypt, much of their time is given to reconverting the Copts, and though these are nominal Christians, and indeed represent the oldest branch of the Christian Church, no one who knows them will deny that this is a good work, or that they do not stand in need of reconversion.

The Bibles and the liturgies used in these old world churches are all written in Coptic, the great-grandchild of the ancient Egyptian language. This has become almost an unknown tongue among the people, who all speak Arabic; and it is

The Missionaries

not even understood by many of their priests.

Their religion, in consequence, has become a mere form. But even yet its spirit is not entirely dead, since many of them are willing to be reconverted, and the missionaries who work among them are meeting already with quite an encouraging success.

The Brahman and the Parsi are as hard to convert as the Moslem. And their religions furnish them with arguments as strong and more subtle than ours.

I do not deny that there are nominal conversions from all these religions, and it is the names of these converts which are sent home in triumph by the less conscientious of the missionaries, to prove that they are earning their salaries. But these conversions are entirely due to interested motives on the part of the converts, and are no subject of congratulation to the missionaries, but rather one of shame, as

A Key to the Orient

being too often open to the imputation of bribery and corruption. This is principally the case in the British oriental possessions, where the subjects soon learn the lesson of hypocrisy from their masters.

The missionary recommends the convert for some small official position, or it may be merely for some labor on government works, and the petition, which would be refused to the " heathen," is always granted to the convert; and this is a notorious fact. Any one who knows the oriental character, knows that the religion of an oriental is so much part of himself that if he gives it up it is not to take another in its place, but to give up all religion.

Such conversions are very dangerous, and very much to be deplored, and we should stop and think whether we are doing good or harm in our missionary endeavor, and remember that Hell is paved with good intentions.

I think the missionaries should and

The Missionaries

would meet with more success among the savages, were it not for two points, which they always make at the beginning of their ministry, and which generally prove a hopeless stumbling block.

The first is that the savages must be clothed, and the second is that they must give up polygamy. In my humble opinion, the first point is a great and unnecessary mistake. The early Christians indeed insisted on every one's being clothed, because the human form had almost become an object of worship with the Greeks and Romans, and nudity belonged inseparably to their heathen rites.

But the savages are different. Their climate makes clothing superfluous; they and their ancestors have arrayed themselves in a few shells and beads and feathers from time immemorial, and to suggest to them that their costume is immodest and wrong, seems to me to instil evil into their minds, rather than good.

A Key to the Orient

The question of polygamy is more serious, and one which I must leave to be decided by some one else. But in the mean time the Mohammedans, who also send missionaries to Africa, and who only restrict the number of wives to four, are quietly but surely gaining all these souls to Islam.

It seems to me that the brightest prospects for the missionaries are in Japan.

The Japanese are a progressive, a friendly, and a most intelligent people, and more than all this they are ready for a new religion.

Buddhism is dead in the hearts of the people, if indeed it ever was alive. Many people may criticise me for saying this, for Buddha has many admirers. Perhaps I am wrong, but Buddhism to me has never seemed a religion at all, but merely a philosophy. One may find in it the resignation to die, but there is nothing in its teachings which can help one to live.

The Missionaries

If we must give it the name of a religion at all, it is only the religion of despair.

Christ has commanded us to go and preach the Gospel to all men. The divine command must be obeyed, but let us stop for a moment and think what mistakes are being made and how they may be rectified.

Max Müller says that the failure of the missionaries is owing to the fact that they are not satisfied to make Christians, they want to make English Christians.

Mrs. Sheldon considers that the great stumbling block in the path is the fact that the missionaries, and Christians in general, do not practise what they preach. This is undoubtedly true to a great extent, and what is more, such a creed of " not deeds but words " means more to people of other faiths than it does to us.

Our religion is the highest and the most difficult to follow; more has been

A Key to the Orient

given to us and more will be asked in return. But we must admit that the believers in general in other religions live up to them better than we live up to ours.

We have one commandment, "Thou shalt not take the name of the Lord thy God in vain." What is it that they whom we call heathen hear oftenest in a Christian colony (so-called), that even the parrots learn from us first, an oath!

A great Christian nation goes to war with China to force upon her the opium trade, — the opium trade, which means ruin and death to millions!

Afterwards they send missionaries to convert them. Is it any wonder that they find it difficult to convince the Chinese that our religion is better than theirs?

But more than all these things, the great cause of the missionaries' failure is their want of unity.

Sent by all denominations as they are, and at war with each other, they come

The Missionaries

before the heathen as Catholics, Episcopalians, Presbyterians, Methodists, and Baptists, not as Christians.

One teaches "free will," another "predestination;" one "infant baptism," another "immersion;" one "damnation of the unbaptized," another "eternal hope;" one "transubstantiation," a second "real presence," and a third that the sacrament means nothing at all.

All these points of doctrine are insisted upon as necessary to salvation, and the bewildered heathen are offered the unedifying spectacle of a church divided against itself, — a spectacle which hopelessly confuses the savage mind and inspires the learned and cultivated heathen with contempt for both us and our faith.

Here again the Moslem missionaries have the advantage of us. Come they from Morocco, Arabia, Persia, Turkistan, from no matter where, they come hand in hand. Each plants the crescent,

A Key to the Orient

and each teaches the same simple creed, "There is no God but Allah, and Mohammed is his Prophet."

More blood has been shed by Christians against each other, and in the name of Christ, than in all other religions that the world has ever seen.

And even now, in this enlightened age, were not peace kept between them by the Moslem, the different sects would tear each other limb from limb around the Holy Sepulchre.

Saladin advised Richard Cœur de Lion to "Conquer the other half of his poor Island before he came to fight in Palestine."

And we would do better, before we set out to teach the heathen, to decide on our belief among ourselves.

Christ has said, "On this rock I will build my Church," not "my Churches."

A Bird's-Eye View of the Religions of the Orient

A BIRD'S-EYE VIEW OF THE RELIGIONS OF THE ORIENT

"IF the Indians had formed their notions of Christianity from the soldiers of Cortez and Pizarro, or if the Hindus had studied the principles of Christian morality in the lives of Clive and Warren Hastings; or, to take a less extreme case, if a Mohammedan, settled in England, were to test the practical working of Christian charity by the spirit displayed in the journals of our religious parties, their notions of Christianity would be about as correct as the ideas which thousands of educated Christians entertain of the diabolical character of heathen religion. Even Christianity has been depraved into certain sacrilegious and revolting sects, and if we

A Key to the Orient

claim the right to appeal to the Gospel as the only test by which our faith is to be judged, we must grant a similar privilege to all who possess a written, and as they believe, revealed authority for the articles of their faith."

It is strange but true that many people, no matter how well educated and cultivated they may be in other respects, are, as concerns the religions, the history, and the whole life of the Orient, ignorant and grossly ignorant.

And they are content to remain so, which, in people who take pleasure in being well informed on other subjects, is the most surprising part. They will study theosophy, altruism, or the latest religion invented by Mrs. Humphrey Ward, but they have no time for Zarathustra, Siddartha, Kong Fu Tse, or Mohammed, who have been the lights of the world.

They do not think the Orient interesting, and yet its history is more dramatic, more

Religions of the Orient

thrilling, more intense than anything of ours. Its life is tinged throughout with a subtle enchantment. Its literature is a mine of precious stones, and its religions when really studied give us the key to the whole history of man. It is Max Müller who says:—

"In the history of the world our religion is but one of many; and in order to understand fully the position of Christianity in the history of the world, and its true place among the religions of mankind, we must compare it not with Judaism only, but with the religious aspirations of the whole world, with all in fact that Christianity came either to destroy or to fulfil."

Brahmanism is the oldest of all religions, so old that it has no beginning, and we may trace it back through history and legend to the dawn of time.

Like all other primeval religions, it is a pantheism, and in it the forces of nature — the earth, the sea, the dawn, the day, the

A Key to the Orient

night, the fire, the lightning — all are deified. Its myths are similar to those of Greece and Rome, less beautiful, less graceful, it is true, but higher, purer, nearer the divine. And under this mythology, which has arisen from the poetic nature of the early Aryan race, and is greatly the result of the early Aryan language with its rich flowers of speech, behind this painted screen, stand the real gods of the primeval world, — Brahma the creator, Vishnu the preserver, Siva the destroyer.

The transmigration of souls is an idea which seems inherent in the Aryan mind. Finding its fullest expression in Brahmanism, it appears under various forms in Buddhism and the religions of the Greeks and Romans, Pythagoras having perfected but by no means originated the doctrine of Metempsychosis.

Centuries of Christian teaching have been necessary to eradicate this idea from our minds, and even now we are some-

Religions of the Orient

times startled by finding that it is the belief of children to whom it had certainly never been taught, but in whose little brains it is innate.

And what idea can be more beautiful than that we and all that lives in nature are animated by the divine spark of the eternal essence? Sent out and recalled again, passing through different forms of life, changing but dying not, immortal,

> "Dust into dust, but the pure spirit shall flow
> Back to the burning fountain whence it came,
> A portion of the eternal which shall glow
> Through time and change unquenchably the same."

Brahmanism as we see it now wears the mask of idolatry. With the lapse of centuries, errors and abuses have crept in; Juggernaut, widow-burning, serpent worship, and the Thugs have been the innovations of the last two thousand years. For a thousand years also this oldest of all

A Key to the Orient

religions lay prostrate in the dust; and Buddhism reigned in its stead. A thousand years it lay not dead but sleeping, and then rising again, like the Phœnix, from its own ashes it drove Buddhism, the democratic intruder, out of India, and resumed its place in the temple and on the throne.

And what wonder if in these thousand years of slavery it lost something of its purity and beauty? Still it is changed, but it is not dead. The mass of its votaries may perhaps be called idolaters; but the Brahmans themselves have lost nothing of its early truth, and their sacred books, the Vedas, whose spirit is not merely noble but high and holy, are still unchanged.

Looking forward it may vanish and be lost; what has had no beginning may have an end, but Brahmanism *was* a pure and beautiful religion in the morning of the world.

And now to the first of the prophets, Zarathustra Spitama, more commonly

Religions of the Orient

known by his Latin name of Zoroaster, or his Persian one of Zerdusht, from the twilight of Indian pantheism, from the sound of falling water and the glimmering green of the jungle, to the snow clad mountains of Iran and the sunrise of monotheism!

Zarathustra Spitama, the first of the Prophets, was born in Bactria, the most eastern province of Iran, in the reign of Kava Vistaspa (Kai Gushtasp), the fifteenth in the line of the Pischdanian Kings.

There is much disagreement about his date, Max Müller making him the contemporary of Abraham, and some writers placing the Pischdanian dynasty immediately before Cyaxares and Cyrus. But on the evidence of language, and the testimony of the best authorities, we may hold that he lived in the middle of the fifteenth century B. C.

Brahmanism, of which Zarathustra was

A Key to the Orient

a priest, was at that time the religion of Iran; but though the world had accepted it without question, and knew nothing better, no pantheism could satisfy the soul of Zarathustra. Determined to meditate and evolve the eternal truth, he retired to a cave in the mountains, lived there as a hermit for eight years, and then reappeared among men, boldly decrying the Deva worship, and proclaiming Ahura Mazda the one god through the cities of Iran.

The world was startled, hearing for the first time from the lips of Zarathustra the name of its God. Men turned to him as flowers toward the sun; the Devas fled before him, with their priests, like shadows. Innumerable converts crowded around him, and among them Isfendiar, the son of Gushtasp and heir to the throne, espoused his cause.

First the son and then the father. Gushtasp embraced the Mazda Yacna religion. Brahmanism was banished be-

Religions of the Orient

yond the mountains to India, and the new faith was established with all its hierarchy of priests, Dastuers, Mobeds, and Hybrids, a thing which, like Minerva, had sprung to life full grown and in armor. And in Rhaga, created the religious Capital, Zarathustra Spitama held sway, Primate of Iran.

The progress of religion is usually slow. Christianity took three hundred years to become the state religion of the Roman Empire. A religion triumphant in the life time of the founder has been the achievement of Zarathustra and Mohammed alone in the history of the world. The Mazda Yacna religion is the purest monotheism. Ahuromazda (living wise spirit) is the one God, embodying in one the principles of good and evil, as whose symbol Zarathustra, abhorring images and idols, has chosen fire.

"The bright spirit appearing in the blazing flame and the presence of the dark

A Key to the Orient

one marked by the wood converted into ashes."

This, of course, is what has caused the Parsis to be branded among their enemies by the name of fire-worshippers. But all who know anything of the real religion know that the sacred fire always burning on their altars is only the Symbol of God.

Then came the Amesha Spenti, called the six councillors of God, in reality the six attributes of the Most High, and not to be considered as anything more than abstract ideas. These are the Vohu Mano (Divine Wisdom); Ardibehest (light), which signifies the omnipresence of God; Sharaver (Divine Mercy in bestowing good gifts); Issandarmat (Devotion) is the symbol of the pure heart; and Khorda and Ameredat preside over vegetation and the fruits of the earth, agriculture being considered by Zarathustra not only as a religious duty but as the first principle of civilization.

Religions of the Orient

And last comes the Archangel Shraosha, who is considered to be the Zarathustrian liturgy standing between God and men.

Zarathustra believed in the old theory of the eternal essence animating all nature, — and surely nothing can be more beautiful, — but discards the doctrine of the transmigration of souls teaching instead our own of heaven and hell.

Hell, the dark abyss into which the lost soul trying to cross the bridge Kinvat which spans the chasm between this world and the next slips and falls, and heaven, "The Paradise of the stars without beginning."

Zarathustra has laid down for his followers six great precepts: truth, and the abhorrence of the lie; prayer, and its universal efficacy; religious toleration; regard for human life; marriage, and the absolute prohibition of celibacy; and the command to enjoy and make the most of the good gifts which God has given us,

A Key to the Orient

and the world which He has made so fair and beautiful.

Zarathustra's moral philosophy forms a triad of thought, word, and deed; and he believes that no man is truly virtuous unless in all these he is good and pure. And forgiveness of sins he teaches is to be obtained by repentance alone.

His speculative philosophy teaches that everywhere in the world a duality exists between good and evil. I will quote from his own words as follows:—

"In the universe there are, from the beginning, two spirits at work, the one making life, the other destroying it. Only this life becomes a prey to death, but not that hereafter over which the destructive spirit has no power." And he teaches always the ultimate triumph of good.

Zarathustra has also taught the existence of angels and devils like our own. In Brahmanism the gods are called Devas, and the evil spirits, Asuras. Zarathustra

Religions of the Orient

calls his devils Devas (from which comes our word), and his angels, Ahuras (" s " in Sanskrit changing into " h " in Zend).

One thing only he has really retained,—the sacred plant, the yellow Soma (Sanskrit), Homa (Zend), and more he tells us of the white or heavenly Homa which blooms in Paradise.

The doctrine of the one God, combining the principles of good and evil, was too difficult, too high and pure to last long untarnished in the human mind. In the reign of Darius Hystaspes, removed from Zarathustra by one thousand years, we find Ahuromazda resolved into a shadowy All Father, and known as Mithra; while the principles of good and evil, now separated and carrying on the war of the Universe, are Ormuzd and Ahiriman.

From a monotheism it has become a dualism; but in none other of its high and holy principles, in nothing else of its purity and beauty, is it changed.

A Key to the Orient

Zarathustra Spitama has but three million followers to-day, and they are nearly all in India, his religion having been driven out of Persia by the victorious sword of Islam. Three millions, — but they hold fast their faith as do the Hebrews theirs; and noted everywhere, where they are known, for their probity, and the purity and beauty of their lives, they have lived up to and justified their religion to the rest of the world for three and thirty centuries.

Siddartha, known as Buddha (the sage), who comes next on our list, I will dismiss in as few words as possible, for of all the founders of the oriental religions he is the only one with whom, or with whose teachings, I have no sympathy.

Every one knows the history of Prince Gautama. Born in the sixth century before Christ, the son of an Indian king, he renounced the world and its splendors and pleasures, and abandoned his palace, to lead,

Religions of the Orient

first, the life of a hermit, and then that of a wandering preacher of a new religion.

The theme is a dramatic one, and has been idealized by Sir Edwin Arnold, Wallace, and others. The veil of distance lends Siddartha enchantment, but the real reason why Buddhism has become lately so popular is, that this is not a religious age, and Buddhism is not a religion.

Siddartha was an *atheist* and a *socialist*, a *nihilist twenty-four centuries before his time.*

He teaches that there is no God, no soul, no future life, no heaven, no hell; that nothing really is, as all things are forever undergoing change; that all existence is evil, and that the only thing to be desired is annihilation.

It seems incredible that in a land of light and beauty like India, any converts to such a creed could have been found, especially as it was as forbidding and disagreeable in practice as in theory, being the most absolute asceticism. The Buddhist must renounce all the pleasures and comforts, the beauties and joys, the passions and desires of life, and devote himself to meditation and the contemplation of the unexplained, which is the only term I can use, as nothing really existed, and *there was nothing*.

Were this absorption complete, the disciple had attained Nirvana. For the first time the world heard the doctrine of celibacy from the lips of Siddartha; and, against nature as this was, it took root, and, for the first time in history, there sprang up monasteries of monks, and the caves of the mountains were peopled by hermits.

For two hundred and fifty years after its birth, Buddhism was accepted only among the lower classes; but about 300 B. C. it was embraced by the Emperor Asoka, and became the state religion of India for a thousand years. At the end of that time it was driven out root and

Religions of the Orient

branch, and sought refuge in Ceylon, Farther India, China, and Japan.

The real reason of the success of Buddhism was a sordid one. The Hindus are not fond of work, and all those who embraced the religious life became ambulant beggars, and were supported by the alms of the believers. Asoka was the grandson of the upstart Shandragupta, and realizing that his low origin deprived him of the sympathy and support of the Brahmans, he overturned their religion and replaced it by the plebeian Buddhism, in which he recognized his natural ally.

As for Buddha himself. It is true that he taught principles of good morality, — such as not to lie, steal, etc.; but all this had been taught by Brahmanism from the beginning, and what he originated was nothing but the blackest pessimism.

As a king, he might have made hundreds of people happy; but he preferred to make millions miserable by depriving them of

A Key to the Orient

all happiness in this world, and all hope in the next.

The most simple conclusion that we can reach, after considering all the circumstances, is, that Prince Gautama was a nervous dyspeptic, and his whole system of philosophy may be summed up in the one cry of hopeless despair, —

We cannot all be happy, therefore let us all be miserable.

Our geographies inform us that one third of the human race are Buddhists, but no more erroneous statement has ever been allowed to stand in print. In China, the religion of Kong Fu Tse is the state religion, and counts among its followers the aristocracy and fully one third of the people, while another third follows Laotse. In Japan, a large proportion of the people are Shintos; and even where Buddhism still exists, it is so changed that Siddartha would hardly recognize its teachings as his own.

Religions of the Orient

Nirvana has been turned into Heaven, and the Burmese and Siamese have returned to the belief in the transmigration of souls, and have invented themselves, besides, a series of hells. No one has yet presumed to invent a God, but the Chinese worship the spirits of their ancestors, and Buddha himself has become almost a Deity.

The truth is, that Buddhism was a belief which no one, outside a hermitage or perhaps a monastery, could follow; and, like all things false, it held in itself from the first the seeds of its own destruction.

The sun of Buddhism is setting; it is changing, fading, dying, and now of all its empire there is left but one last real stronghold of this faith, or far more unfaith, Ceylon.

This, too, must yield to time and the inevitable, and soon or late Prince Gautama, and his phantom religion, will be consigned forever to Nirvana.

A Key to the Orient

And now let us turn from the nihilist to the great conservative, Kong Fu Tse (Latin Confucius), who was born in China, 551 B. C., of the noble family of Khung.

Asia has been the mother of all religions, and it is a fact worthy of note that the founders of all faiths have been men of noble blood.

At the age of twenty-two, Kong Fu Tse appeared as a teacher, and soon gathered around him a throng of disciples. Possessed of many virtues and noble qualities, in conjunction with his gigantic intellect, his great passion was the love of mankind; and the whole effort of his life and teachings was to preserve and increase their happiness.

Though the founder of a religion and a reformer of all evil, he was an ardent conservative and lover of the past.

"I am not one," he says, " who was born in the possession of knowledge. I

Religions of the Orient

am one who is fond of antiquity and earnest in seeking it there."

Of the writings of Kong Fu Tse, though the five Kings are ascribed to him, only the fifth, the Chun Tsew (Spring and Autumn), is really his. The Yih, the Shoo, and the She have been compiled by him from ancient writings; and the Le Ke is considered to be the work of his disciples.

The wisdom of Kong Fu Tse has the irresistible charm of simple truth, and his maxims are as pure and sweet as old-time garden-flowers.

"The superior man is catholic and no partisan; the mean man is partisan and no catholic."

"To see what is right and not do it is want of courage."

"Do ye unto others as ye would that others should do unto you."

Confucius taught four things: Letters, Ethics, Devotion of the Soul, and Truth-

A Key to the Orient

fulness. He believed in the immortality of the soul, but was loath to speak of the life hereafter.

When urged to tell of death he replied, "Let us know what life is first."

Kong Fu Tse died in 478 B.C. complaining, though he had many followers, that not one of the princes of the empire would adopt his faith.

Two generations later his name had become a power, — a power ever increasing. To-day he counts his followers by millions, and his impress is marked indelibly in the whole national character of China, the largest empire of the world.

And now to the last of the Prophets and the latest of all the great religions of the world.

All hail, Mohammed! Prophet of God or not, still greatest and most wonderful of men.

Christianity had been the state religion of the Roman Empire for three hundred

Religions of the Orient

years; but the Church was already distracted by contending sects, and the world was at its darkest when the moon of Islam rose.

No man who has ever lived has been so slandered and misrepresented as Mohammed. Until the last century he was known to Europe only through the reports of his enemies, and no lie that could be invented about him and his teachings has been left untold.

And even now many otherwise enlightened people entertain a mediæval prejudice against him and his religion, which is unworthy of themselves and the age.

The usual reproach which is made against Mohammed is that he permitted polygamy. Let us dismiss this at once before we speak of his religious teachings, with which it has nothing whatever to do. Polygamy has been the custom of all oriental nations from time immemorial, and the only action of Mohammed in the

A Key to the Orient

matter was to limit the number of wives to four. He also strove to render divorce more difficult, and gave women rights of property and dower; and he improved their condition in every way in his power.

It is true that he gave female slaves to their masters. But we must remember that his religion was founded on the Old Testament, which for this gave him full authority; and he decreed, furthermore, that all children, whether born of wife or slave, should be legitimate and equal in their rights.

It is always easy to find motes in our neighbor's eyes; but those who are horror-stricken at the social system of Mohammed, should not forget that there are weak points in ours. The immoral class, which in spite of all the teachings of Christianity, plays so large a part in all Christian lands, is almost unknown in Islam, and there are, beyond a doubt, more women who live by immorality in London or

Religions of the Orient

Paris than in the whole Ottoman Empire, from Morocco to Turkistan.

As to the absurd idea that Mohammed denied women souls, it is like the rest, a pure invention. Mohammed promised paradise and eternal youth and happiness to women, on the one condition of their being mothers and fulfilling their destiny in this world.

Mohammed, born in 571 A. D., belonged to the most noble family of Arabia, that of El Hashim, and his grandfather, Abd el Multalib, was the hereditary Prince of Mecca and guardian of the Kaba.

His father, Abdallah, who was a younger son, was the handsomest and most attractive young man in Mecca, and tradition relates that two hundred virgins died of jealousy and despair on the night in which he married the beautiful Amina, Mohammed's mother. The beauty and magnetic charm of his parents descended

A Key to the Orient

to Mohammed, and no doubt bore their part in his wonderful power of winning hearts.

Losing his father before his birth, and his mother in infancy, the first years of Mohammed were spent with his wet nurse, Halima, in the desert; and indeed, as he later became the leader of a caravan, we may say, that throughout life the desert, with its mirage, its silence, and its mystery, was his home.

Married at the age of twenty-six to the widow Kadijah, who proved herself a true wife and noble woman, Mohammed lived till in his fortieth year the life of other men.

Then suddenly he began to speak, and, with more than mortal courage as it seemed, to denounce the idols of his people, and to proclaim Allah the only God.

But at first he spoke in vain. Arabia was steeped in a mixture of Sabeanism, which had been its ancient religion, and a

Religions of the Orient

later and more degraded idolatry. The Arabs were wed to their idols; and, in their indignation at his teachings, only the influence of his uncle, Abu Talib, saved Mohammed from death.

Forced to fly to the desert, we see him persecuted, hunted, and in danger of death. Then a sudden change of fortune, and he enters Medina in triumph, like a king.

Then strife and the clouds of civil war, and then victory, — the victory of truth over error, of morning over night. And we see the men of Mecca bearing palm branches to Medina, kneeling at the feet of Mohammed and hailing him Lord of Arabia and Prophet of God.

Not only did Mohammed annihilate idolatry in Arabia, but with it the two great vices of his people, drunkenness and gambling. No other man has done as much in the history of the world. And that he has kept not only his own, but all succeeding generations of his followers from their favorite sins, — for the Mussulmans who drink and gamble are only the exceptions that prove the rule, — shows how unparalleled his influence on the human race has been and is.

No other man has understood human nature as Mohammed has done; and this knowledge, combined with his genius, has given him his more than mortal power.

The first principle and meaning of Islam is resignation to the will of God; and all those who are thus resigned, no matter what their religion, are Moslems at heart. Founding his teachings on the Bible, Mohammed reiterated the Ten Commandments, and taught that there had been four great prophets, of whom he was the last and greatest. The other three are Moses, David, and Jesus, who is called Issa ben Marian the prophet, but not the Son of God.

Five great precepts are laid down, some-

Religions of the Orient

times symbolized by the five fingers of the hand: prayer, almsgiving, fasting, cleanliness, and war against the infidels, for the purpose of spreading through all the world the faith of Islam.

Then comes the equality of all men in the sight of God. But let no one suppose that Mohammed believed in the chimera of social equality. God has made social distinctions, and one man is born a prince and another a peasant. Different duties have been assigned them in life, but their positions are equally honorable. The inferior must treat his superior with deference and respect, and the superior his inferior with kindness and consideration. Every one must do his best in his own sphere; and if he rises from a lowly to a high position, there must be no prejudice against him on account of his former state, for no man may choose the position in which he shall be born, but is assigned thereto by the will of God.

A Key to the Orient

This is undoubtedly what gives the Moslem of the most humble as well as of the highest rank that innate dignity and self-respect which distinguish him from the rest of the world. And this it is which has made and will always make the hydra of socialism unknown in Islam.

It has been the fate of most religions to change and degenerate with the lapse of time. Christianity itself, the broad straight river of truth, has split into a thousand channels, and the Church which Christ founded on the rock is named no longer, alas, one, but legion.

More than twelve centuries have passed since the death of Mohammed, but it is the proud boast of Islam, that she alone of all religions has undergone no change.[1]

---

[1] There is one great schism in Islam, that of the Shias; but it is a political, and not a religious difference, founded on the succession of the Kalifs.

The Shias contend that Ali alone was the legiti-

Religions of the Orient

Dynasties have risen and fallen, earthquakes and plagues and famines have passed by, and the old world has given place to the new. But still, as the first Muezzin called to prayer from the first Minaret, his successors call to prayer today; from Morocco to Turkistan — "There is no God but Allah, and Mohammed is his Prophet."

mate successor of Mohammed, while the Sonnites (the Orthodox) maintain that the succession as it occurred, of Abu Bekr, Omar Othman, and Ali, was just and ordained of God. This schism reigns in Persia, whence the hatred between the Persians and the Arabs and Turks. Its followers may be known by the black fez which they wear to distinguish them from the Sonnites, who wear the red, thereby proclaiming themselves orthodox, and acknowledging the Sultan of Turkey as the successor of the Prophet and ruler of Islam.

The Religion of Zarathustra Spitama

This essay was my first oriental effort. This study of the Zoroastrian religion has made some progress since it was written, and I, too, have learned more. But I let it stand as it is, out of a little feeling for myself, and beg a gentle criticism for the work of a girl of eighteen.

THE RELIGION OF ZARA-THUSTRA SPITAMA

THE STAR OF THE MAGI

"Not vainly did the ancient Persian make
   His altar the high places and the peak
Of earth o'er gazing mountains, and thus take
   A fit and unwalled temple, there to seek
The Spirit, in whose honor shrines are weak,
   Upreared of human hands. Come and compare
Columns and idol dwellings, Goth or Greek,
   With Nature's realms of worship, earth and air."

RELIGION is a study not only very beautiful and interesting, but also of the greatest importance, being so intimately blended with history and philology that the three are almost inseparable. And if we seek to know the people of antiquity, and to understand how they looked at life, and what they felt, the best

A Key to the Orient

answer to our question lies in what they believed.

Much interest is felt at present in Buddhism, and everything written on the subject is received with favor.

It is this that emboldens me to offer this slight sketch of the religion of Zoroaster, far older and more beautiful, though not now so widely spread as that of the royal Gautama. And I make the effort, unworthy as it is, in the hope that others may be led to study the subject for themselves.

The flash and roar of the cannon are like lightning and thunder, but it is the spark that lights the train.

The Zoroastrian Mazda Yacna religion was unknown in Europe a hundred and fifty years ago.

Some Parsi manuscripts had indeed been brought to England from India in the seventeenth century, but for want of a key to the languages in which they were

Religion of Zarathustra Spitama

written, Pahlavi and Zend, they remained for a long time a sealed book.

In the year 1700, the great Oxford scholar, Hyde, attempted a treatise on the subject, but knowing really nothing of what he was writing about, this is not deserving of notice.

The glorious discovery of the real teachings of Zarathustra Spitama was destined to be made in France.

In the middle of the century, Anquetil du Perron, a young Frenchman, happened to see in the Bodleian library a facsimile of a few pages of the Zend-avesta. Being of an inquiring turn of mind, he determined to know what they meant or perish in the attempt.

With this end in view he resolved to go to India; and, no other opportunity offering, he shipped as a sailor on board a vessel belonging to the East India company.

His perseverance was however rewarded; for the government, hearing of the affair,

A Key to the Orient

released him from this engagement, paid his passage to India, and furnished him with a pension by means of which to prosecute his studies while there.

Du Perron sailed in 1754, and on arriving spent some time travelling about in search of the information he desired.

The undertaking was much more difficult than he had imagined. The Mobeds and Dastuers (Parsi priests), not understanding his motive in prying into their religion, treated him with the greatest distrust.

At last the Dastuer Darab at Curat agreed for a certain sum of money to instruct him in the Zend and Pahlavi languages, and to furnish him with the necessary manuscripts.

Du Perron commenced to study with the greatest enthusiasm and (overlooking the fact that the Dastuer's knowledge of the sacred languages was very imperfect, and that he himself was not too well

Religion of Zarathustra Spitama

versed in the modern Sanskrit, which was their medium of communication) convinced himself in a couple of years that he had mastered Pahlavi and Zend.

In 1759 he returned to Europe, bringing with him a hundred and eight Parsi manuscripts, and two years later published his translation of the Zend-avesta, which, though full of faults and inaccuracies, was received with the greatest enthusiasm throughout France.

The English, naturally adverse to everything French, treated Du Perron's translation very coldly; and Sir William Jones published an essay in which he stigmatized the whole thing as nonsense, and boldly denied the existence of any such languages as Pahlavi and Zend.

The Germans, slower in their judgment, now took up the subject; and the great Danish scholar Rasksoon proved the sacred languages to be pure Aryan dialects, tracing them back from the Persian

A Key to the Orient

to the Median, and thence to the Bactrian, which leads directly to the classical Zend.

This course was however a very difficult one to follow, and it was not until Eugene Bournouf, Professor of the College of France at Paris, thought of reaching the Zend through her sister, the Sanskrit of the Vedas, instead of by the successive steps of her Iranian daughters, that anything further was achieved.

This attempt proved very successful, more especially as a Sanskrit translation of the Parsi prayer-book, the Yasna (which contains the writings of Zarathustra Spitama himself), was found.

Bournouf's labors were cut short by death; but his excellent commentary on the Yasna still ranks with anything that has been produced, and contributes even more than the work of Du Perron to give the glory of this great discovery to France.

For the last forty or fifty years the work has been carried on slowly but

Religion of Zarathustra Spitama

steadily in Germany, and we have now two translations of the Zend-avesta and one of the Gathas.

The first of these, by Friedrich Spiegel, Professor of Oriental Languages at the Bavarian University of Erlangen, is almost as incorrect as that of Du Perron, being written carelessly and hurriedly, and without any real appreciation of the subject.

The only true and correct version of the Zend-avesta is that of Westergaard, Professor at Copenhagen, who visited Persia and India in pursuit of information, and who is far too conscientious to set before the public anything which he is unable to prove.

Last came the Gathas, translated by Haug, the oldest and most beautiful portion of all the sacred writings of the Parsis,— a translation which may be taken without reservation, because the author is animated not only by a great appreciation of his subject, but also by an infinite love

A Key to the Orient

for the venerable religion which was once the light of the world.

Zoroastrianism was known to the early Greeks as the doctrine of the Magi, and greatly respected by them.

The earliest writers on the subject were Ktesias, 400 B.C., Deinon, 350 B.C., Theopompos of Chios, 300 B.C., and Hermippos of Smyrna, 250 B.C.

These writings are nearly all lost, but the opinions of Hermippos, who appears to have been the only one possessed of any real knowledge, have been preserved by Plutarch in his "Isis and Osiris."

Our earliest account of the Zoroastrian Mazda Yacna religion is to be found in the works of Herodotus, written 450 B.C.

In his own words, "I know that the Persians observe these customs. It is not customary among them to have idols made, temples built, or altars erected; they even upbraid with folly those who do so. I can account for that only from their not

Religion of Zarathustra Spitama

believing that the gods are men as the Hellenes do. They are accustomed to bring sacrifices to Zeus on the summits of mountains; they call the whole celestial circle Zeus."

"The sacrificer ought not to pray only for his own prosperity; he must also pray for the welfare of all Persians, and for the king, because he is included among them."

"Lying is regarded as the most discreditable thing by them; next to it, incurring debt, chiefly because the debtor is often compelled to tell lies."

The Mohammedan writers have also interested themselves in this religion, the believers in which fell under their yoke at the conquest of Persia; and it has been treated by them with great liberality.

Sharastani, a celebrated sage who lived about the year 1100, classifies the Parsis with the Mussulmans and Christians; and many of their writers identify Zoroaster with Abraham.

A Key to the Orient

To the Jews, this religion was probably well known through their frequent intercourse with the Persians.

It is hinted at in Ezekiel viii. 16, 17, and, from the way in which Cyrus the Great is spoken of by the Prophet Isaiah, we are led to infer that the doctrines of Zoroaster were not so diametrically opposed to the Mosaic creed.

Indeed there are a great many points of similarity, and the two beliefs in the devil and the resurrection of the dead are so exactly alike that it is impossible not to consider their source the same.

The word paradise has no existence in Hebrew, and was unmistakably borrowed from the Zend; and the way in which the one God names Himself is the same in both cases (to Moses in the one, in the other to Zoroaster), "Ayeh asher ayeh" in Hebrew, "Amhi yat Amhi" in Zend, "I am who I am."

The date of the founder of this religion,

Religion of Zarathustra Spitama

Zarathustra Spitama, better known by his Latin name of Zoroaster, is in dispute. It has been a common error to place him five hundred years B. C., in the time of Hystaspes, the father of the winged Darius; but this is utterly incorrect, and rests on nothing but the fact that he lived in the reign of a king named Vistaspa.

The Greek writers are disposed to place him four thousand years before the Christian Era. This is evidently going too far; but when we consider that the stupendous Parsi literature, of which Zarathustra Spitama laid the corner-stone, was complete four hundred years B. C., and compare it with the Hebrew literature, whose growth occupied two thousand five hundred years, we cannot allow a less time for its compilation than a thousand years.

It is therefore impossible to assign Zarathustra Spitama a later date than fourteen hundred years B. C., thereby proving

A Key to the Orient

him to have been at least contemporary with Moses.

At all events, it was not only long anterior to the rise of Buddhism, but even to the immigration of the Brahmans to India, for we find that the Deva religion, not differing essentially from modern Brahmanism, was then the established faith of Bactria, and Zarathustra Spitama himself one of the Deva priests.

After serving in this capacity for some time, Zarathustra, a man of wonderful mental powers and intellect far beyond his time, became convinced of the falsity of the polytheistic religion of the Devas, and, inspired by a longing for the truth, resigned his office and retired from the world.

During the eight years that followed, Zarathustra lived like a hermit in a cave, spending his time in meditation, and, as his disciples believe, visited by angels, and receiving revelations from the one only God whose being he was destined to reveal.

Religion of Zarathustra Spitama

At the end of that time he re-appeared among his countrymen, and announced to them the Mazda Yacna religion.

His teachings, which were at once embraced by Vistaspa, the king, spread like wildfire through all Bactria; and the few remaining adherents of the Deva religion were forced to the south and east, and finally across the mountains into India.

Zarathustra then established himself at Ragha, a city which thenceforward was exempted from the rule of the king, and governed by his successors, the high priests, taking the name of Zarathustrian Ragha.

The wonderful success of the Mazda Yacna religion, which is unparalleled in history, was due not only to its sublime character, but to its purity and truth.

The doctrine of Zarathustra Spitama, though since corrupted by innovations from the old Deva and Sabean faiths, was the purest possible monotheism.

He believed in one eternal God,—

A Key to the Orient

Ahuromazda (living wise spirit), embodying in one the principles of good and evil, Cpenta Mainyus and Angro Mainyus, as the symbol of whom he takes fire.

"The bright spirit appearing in the blazing flame, and the presence of the dark one marked by the wood converted into charcoal."

The only other personation in this theology is the Archangel Shraosha, who is supposed to stand between God and man.

Then there are six attributes of the Most High, which are dignified by the name of Heavenly Councillors, but are not to be regarded as anything more than abstract ideas.

These are: first, the Vohu Mano (good mind), a portion of the divine wisdom given to all men to instruct them, if they will listen to its promptings, in the right.

The second is Ardibehest (light), which signifies the omnipresence of God, and

Religion of Zarathustra Spitama

also that the sun and moon and stars, fire, and whatever else is radiant, shine only through his light.

Sharaver, the third, which signifies wealth and the mercy of Ahuromazda in bestowing on his followers all good gifts.

The fourth, Issandarmat (devotion), is a symbol of the pure heart of the true Ahuromazda worshipper.

Khorda and Ameredat, the fifth and sixth, preside over vegetation and the fruits of the earth, agriculture being considered by Zarathustra not only as a religious duty, but as the first principle of civilization.

Zarathustra's speculative philosophy, which must not be confounded with his theology, constitutes a dualism as set forth in his own words.

" 1. Everywhere in the world a duality is to be perceived, such as the good and the evil, light and darkness, this life and that life, human wisdom and divine wisdom.

A Key to the Orient

" 2. In the universe there are from the beginning two spirits at work, the one making life, the other destroying it.

" 3. Only this life becomes a prey to death, but not that hereafter, over which the destructive spirit has no power.

" 4. The principal duty of man is to obey the word and commandments of God.

" 5. The divine Spirit cannot be resisted.

" 6. God exercises his rule in the world through the works prompted by the divine Spirit, who is working in man and nature.

" 7. Men should pray to God and worship him, he hears the prayers of the good.

" 8. The Soul of the pure will hereafter enjoy everlasting life, that of the wicked will have to undergo everlasting punishment.

" 9. All good creatures are Ahuromazdas. He is the reality of the good mind, word, and deed."

Religion of Zarathustra Spitama

Zarathustra's moral philosophy forms a trilogy of thought, word, and deed, and he believes that unless in all of these three he is not good and pure, no man can be truly virtuous; and that forgiveness for sins committed is to be obtained by repentance alone.

The Parsi Scriptures, consisting of the writings of Zarathustra Spitama and his disciples and successors, were at one time of such immense extent that at the date of the Macedonian conquest, 353 B.C., they were said to contain 2,000,000 verses.

But, chiefly owing to the five centuries between this event and the succession of the Sassanids, during which period the Mazda Yacna religion was unsupported by any king, and the still more rigorous rule of the Mohammedans, which came later, and partly due no doubt to the carelessness and ignorance of the priests, a great part of it was lost.

A Key to the Orient

We know that the Zenda-vesta proper consisted of twenty-one parts, called nasks, of which only the twentieth, the Vendidad, remains.

A list of the contents of these other nasks has been preserved, from which we learn that they treated not so much of religious subjects, as of medicine, agriculture, astronomy, philosophy, botany, and indeed every branch of literature, and were probably the work of the successive Zarathustras, or high priests.

The Vendidad is a code of rules for purging uncleanness of all sorts, with the exception of the three first fargards.

These, which are evidently of much earlier date, contain a poetical account of the creation, which by some has been attributed to Zarathustra Spitama himself.

The Visparad, which comes next is the liturgy of the Parsis; it contains the invocations to be used at sacrifices, and the services for the festivals at the beginning of the six seasons of the year.

The Yasna is the prayer-book, containing all the Parsi prayers, which indeed are more properly hymns, as they are not to be spoken but chanted.

This, the holiest of all books, consists of three parts, the younger Yasna of unknown date, written in the ordinary language of the Avesta, and the older Yasna, which is written in a more ancient dialect, known as the Gatha.

The younger Yasna consists of fragments of other books and short writings on various subjects. The most important of these are the Homa Yasht, which describes the preparation and drinking of the Homa, and chants the power and praises of the Heavenly Plant, and the Shrosh Yasht, which is dedicated to the Archangel Shraosha, who personifies the whole divine worship of the Mazda Yacna religion. The older Yasna contains the Yasna

A Key to the Orient

Haptanhaiti (the Yasna of the seven chapters) and the most sacred of all Zoroastrian writings, the five "Gathas," which alone of all are beyond doubt the work of Zarathustra.

These Gathas are believed to contain all that was revealed to Zarathustra. The words which head them are of the highest interest. "The revealed thought, the revealed word, the revealed deed of the righteous Zarathustra. The archangels first sang the Gathas!"

I will give a few verses of these wonderful hymns.

"I know thee to be the primeval spirit, thou wise, so high in mind as to create the world, and the father of the Vohu Mano."

"Blessed is he, blessed are all men to whom the living wise God of his own command should grant those two everlasting powers wholesomeness and immortality. For this very good, I beseech thee, Ahuromazda, mayest thou through thy

Religion of Zarathustra Spitama

angel of piety give me happiness, the good true things, and the possession of the Vohu Mano."

"We praise all good thoughts, all good words, all good deeds which are and will be, and we likewise keep clean and pure all that is good."

"We worship Ahuromazda the pure, the master of purity. We worship the Amesha Spentas (angels), the possessors of good. We worship the whole creation of the true Spirit, both the spiritual and the terrestrial, all that supports the welfare of the good creation and the spread of the good Mazda Yacna religion."

The third book, the Khorda Avesta, consists of contributions from the Persian poets in commemoration of the feats of the angels, which were chanted at their festivals corresponding to the Christian Saints days. But these belong to a very much later date, and are only valuable as mythological poems.

A Key to the Orient

One may believe in the inspiration of Zarathustra or not, but without this belief his work and its wonderful success are easily explained and understood.

Zarathustra, with his wonderful intellect and keen insight into things, saw clearly that the religion around him was false.

He engaged in a search after truth, and to those who seek her Truth reveals herself.

Zarathustra felt the light within his soul, and, knowing that there must be a source beyond himself, he turned his face toward the east and waited for the dawn. The dawn broke, the light for which he longed was given; and, pointing to the star which by faith had risen out of darkness, he cried to the world, "Learn the difference between good and evil; these are devils whom ye serve, behold I have found the Truth."

Religion of Zarathustra Spitama.

Tradition, in the Orient often more trustworthy than documentary evidence, related that Zarathustra inspired his followers with the belief that some time the Son of God, a divinity not elsewhere spoken of in his teachings, would come under the form of man and redeem the world.

This idea was not new to the Aryan mind, having been taught by the Brahmans in the doctrine of the Avatars of Vishnu.

But where it was imperfect, for Vishnu only came to *help* mankind, Zarathustra made it perfect, his God coming to *redeem!*

For centuries this idea lingered in the Persian mind like a seed in the earth, and at last put forth a single flower.

The first to adore our Lord Jesus Christ as he lay in the manger was neither Jew nor Roman, but the three Magi, — Zarathustrian priests, who came from a far country, Persia, to worship him whose star they had seen in the east!

www.ingramcontent.com/pod-product-compliance
Lightning Source LLC
Chambersburg PA
CBHW022116160426
43197CB00009B/1053